WHAT PEOPLE A



# FLOURISHIN

We learn and grow in relation to each other. We become, for better or for worse, within a web of relatedness... Appreciative coaching is a fully affirmative approach to human performance and development. It is a shift away from deficit-based assessments of human weaknesses toward strengths-based inquiry into human capabilities, potential and callings. It is a shift away from relating to people through their weaknesses toward seeing all people with noble potential to be discovered, nurtured and expressed.

This book is both a challenge and a way to see people as sources of relationally enacted, positive potential, with ideas, questions and gifts to contribute to the world. It opens the door to a world of appreciation, strengths and positivity in the realm of human performance and development. At the same time, it gently closes the door on theories that posit people as flawed, and in need of management, control and redemption. It is up to you how far you wish to open the door. You may choose to read and apply some of the questions and techniques in this book to your ongoing coaching practice; or you may choose to adopt appreciative coaching fully as your way of relating to people at work and at home.

**Diana Whitney**

## Reviews

I've read Miriam's latest book *Flourishing Together*, and I believe the title of this books says it all. Based on the principles of Appreciative Inquiry this has become a book that explains how we can flourish together. Apart from an introduction to

Appreciative Inquiry and its backgrounds, it focuses on the use of appreciative coaching and how, by bringing relevant others into the coaching process, we create a richer environment for the person being coached. As an experienced coach Miriam takes us through this process in a thorough way, touching on the many aspects of Appreciative Coaching. A wonderful, rich book for any one who would like to explore the world of Appreciative Coaching!
**Joep C. de Jong**

Miriam Subirana is to be admired for her profound insights about human relations. She has written a series of valuable books about what can happen between people. In her latest book *Flourishing Together* she combines this knowledge into an unparalleled reflective experience. Whilst reading, you feel being coached appreciatively. Further reading helps you even to become an appreciative coach yourself. Everyone who buys *Flourishing Together* is a potential contributor to making the world a better place.
**Cees Hoogendijk** (AI practitioner, driven by the "Humanization of Organization")

# Flourishing Together

## Guide to Appreciative Inquiry Coaching

# Flourishing Together

## Guide to Appreciative Inquiry Coaching

Miriam Subirana

Preface by Diana Whitney

BOOKS

Winchester, UK
Washington, USA

First published by O-Books, 2016
O-Books is an imprint of John Hunt Publishing Ltd., Laurel House, Station Approach,
Alresford, Hants, SO24 9JH, UK
office1@jhpbooks.net
www.johnhuntpublishing.com

For distributor details and how to order please visit the 'Ordering' section on our website.



ISBN: 978 1 78535 376 5
Library of Congress Control Number: 2015958988



A CIP catalogue record for this book is available from the British Library.

Original title in Spanish: *Florecer juntos, guía de coaching apreciativo*
Translator, CAROLINE WILSON
Translation paid with the help of Taos Institute

Painting of the cover by Miriam Subirana
"Spring, hope and life" Oil on canvas

Design: Stuart Davies

Printed and bound by CPI Group (UK) Ltd, Croydon, CR0 4YY, UK

# CONTENTS

The seed of joy lies in relationship.

# Preface

We are made and imagined in relation to each other. In the play *My Fair Lady*, Eliza Doolittle says to the Professor, "If you treat me like a flower girl I will become a flower girl. If you treat me like a lady I will become a lady." And so it is for all of us. We learn and grow in relation to each other. We become, for better or for worse, within a web of relatedness. The African term, Ubuntu, which translates to mean, "I am because you are," beautifully illustrates the idea of relational identity.

Coaching is a collaborative process through which coaches and clients learn, make meaning and develop in relation to each other. Appreciative coaching is a fully affirmative approach to human performance and development. It is a shift away from deficit-based assessments of human weaknesses toward strengths-based inquiry into human capabilities, potential and callings. It is a shift away from relating to people through their weaknesses toward seeing all people with noble potential to be discovered, nurtured and expressed.

This idea is especially important when applied to workplaces around the world. Where people are treated as parts of an organizational machine that needs to be managed and controlled, people will behave like disengaged parts of a machine. If they are treated as problems to be solved, with weaknesses to overcome, people will behave in problematic ways. If, on the other hand, leadership and coaching practices treat people as valued contributors, people will more readily engage and contribute. Leadership and coaching practices can either invite and reinforce weaknesses or bring out the best of people and teams. For this reason, coaches, managers and leaders seeking ways to help people discover their strengths and bring their best to work will find this book profoundly useful.

This book is both a challenge and a way to see people as

sources of relationally enacted, positive potential, with ideas, questions and gifts to contribute to the world. It opens the door to a world of appreciation, strengths and positivity in the realm of human performance and development. At the same time, it gently closes the door on theories that posit people as flawed, and in need of management, control and redemption. It is up to you how far you wish to open the door. You may choose to read and apply some of the questions and techniques in this book to your ongoing coaching practice; or you may choose to adopt appreciative coaching fully as your way of relating to people at work and at home.

I invite you to fully take the D.A.R.E offered by this book.

D – Help your clients discover their gifts, strengths, preferred ways of expressing themselves and their calling, that place where their gifts and the world's needs overlap. Appreciative coaching helps people discover whom they are at their best in relation to the people and situations that matter to them.

A – Help people to apply their strengths and values in service to their families, communities and organizations. Help them to learn from others and adapt best practices to their own ways of working. Appreciative coaching helps people take action, learn, adapt and achieve.

R – Help people reflect upon their performance and the ripples they create in the world. Help people take relational responsibility recognizing that all they say and do affects others in their web of relatedness. Appreciative coaching helps people recognize the footprint they leave on humanity as well as nature. It helps people not just be their best, but also be the best for the world.

E – Help people expand and extend their contribution to the world. Help people explore options for greater service and bolder actions in alignment with their strengths and values. Appreciative coaching helps people explore possibilities and act upon those that make a positive difference.

I can assure you, no matter how far you open the door and accept the challenge this book offers, you and the people you coach will benefit from greater clarity and confidence to courageously live into your dreams.

Diana Whitney
Chapel Hill, NC, USA

November 2014

# Introduction

To live appreciatively is to feel gratitude for everything that life brings me. Whether it is positive or negative, good or bad, I decide to see the positive side that helps me to value, to be thankful and to move forward. I have many reasons to be sad about my past, angry about the things that have happened to me, or fearful of my uncertain future, but I decide consciously to be grateful for the lessons learned. I appreciate what the people who accompanied me on part of my journey contributed to my life, even though we later went our different ways. I decide to live with appreciative lenses and to hold attractive images of the future which strengthen my trust in the present and my courage to move forward through the uncertainty.

Instead of complaining, I decide to be brave and to recognise the oak in the acorn, as Thatchenkery poetically expresses:

> Appreciative Intelligence is the ability to see the mighty oak in the acorn. Metaphorically, it is the ability to see more than the present existence of a small capped nut. It is the capacity to see a strong trunk and countless leaves as emerging from the nut as time unfolds. It is the ability to see a breakthrough product, top talent, or valuable solution for the future that is currently hidden in the present situation.[1]

I have decided to write this book because I am convinced of the value that appreciative inquiry and appreciative coaching contributes to the development and growth of people and teams, and the positive impact they have on their network of relationships. Appreciative inquiry is a life philosophy, a methodology and a process that focuses on the best of people and relationships, driving change through bringing out the strengths of people and organisations. I have already written at length on the subject in my book, written with David Cooperrider, *Indagación Apreciativa: Un enfoque innovador para la transformación personal y de las organizaciones. Inspirémonos para diseñar nuestro futuro.*

Appreciative coaching nourishes that which gives us life and stimulates us to grow. Inspired by the heliotropic principle through which plants grow towards the light, as human beings we advance in the direction of the questions we ask ourselves, towards what we want and the images that attract us to the future.

We live in the reality created by our conversations and by the stories we tell ourselves. So I propose that we have conversations which are generative of inspiring realities opening us to other possibilities, and that we tell ourselves stories which nourish our love of life and our generosity, positive emotions and good experiences. Let us think about other ways of seeing, living and talking about adversity. The words that we use to define problems are negotiable; we can use new languages to move forward.

In this book, I set out some reflections and questions. What essential elements should be taken into consideration in accompanying people? How can we live to our full potential? What is appreciative coaching? How do we ask appreciative questions? What language is appropriate if our conversations are to generate spaces of trust and growth? What enables us to flourish together as human beings? What impact do our relationships and conversations have on what we are?

If you are a coach, this book will give you guidelines in order to introduce appreciative elements into your practice. If you are a leader, manager, or in charge of a group of people, these pages will extend your possibilities for improving the way you lead. If you are a father or mother of a family, the next chapters will guide you so as to improve your ability to bring out the best in your children and support them in what will most make them flourish and shine. As a teacher, you will find ideas to incorporate into your practice, and broaden your vision and perspective, and that of your students.

As a reader, you have in your hands a book that offers you the possibility of travelling paths into the realms of your being you most need to shine a light on. Through questions and reflections I invite you to see your own personal history with new eyes, to be at peace and grateful for your past, in order to live your present with greater wholeness and to trust in your ability to design and create the best future for you and your kin.

Finally, and before you embark on further reading, I want to explain to you that I have struggled to decide what name to give to the person who is accompanied. For me, it is a *person*; however, in the text, I saw that it could create confusion, given that the one who accompanies, the coach, is themselves a person (who accompanies another). For the sake of clarity for the reader, I have decided to use the more widely used term in the world of coaching, which is "client". In the coaching relationship, some call the person being accompanied the *coachee*, but the usage of the word client has become common, due to the fact that a relationship of professional exchange comes into play. You will see that many of the guidelines that I suggest in these chapters can be applied to one's personal life and to accompanying each other in generating moments of wholeness and meaningful relationships. So I hope that if you are looking for guidelines with which to have better relationships, you do not get confused by the use of the word "client", and that you can read the book in such a way that it helps and enriches you.

# Part I

# Accompanying people

Every act of creation drinks from the fountain of Life. Those who connect to that fountain become creative beings. We have in front of us an invitation to unfold all the potential of creative freedom that we have, and it helps us to understand that what is at stake is much more than doing things; it is to turn our very existence into a creative act. To do so we have been brought to existence: to give a unique form to the portion of Life that has been placed in our hands. Being depositaries of the co-creating act of existence like this is permanently made up of two tempos: receiving and giving, taking on and turning one's own life into an offering.
– Javier Melloni[2]

# 1. Opening the door

Accompanying a person in the discovery of themselves, in resolving their crossroads or dispelling their clouds, is both a fascinating task and a big responsibility. In each encounter I continue to be surprised at the great mystery that we are as human beings. In the realms of our being there are many things, much of them unnecessary, such as noise and heavy baggage, incrusted experiences that are difficult to get rid of, but we also find a great capacity for imagination and creativity, and surprisingly, everything that we are looking for and that we need is there. It remains hidden by emotions and dramatic, almost histrionic thoughts, locked up by our fears and doubts. It is so near, less than a millimetre away and requiring less than a second to reach it. However, we travel miles in search of it and years pass until we manage to prise open the door even a tiny way to where the treasure we long for resides.

Day after day I ask myself – What, then, is my responsibility as a coach, as a person who offers herself to accompany you on your search, on your journey through life? As I go forwards, my listening becomes more open and more subtle. From my inner silence, I connect with what the other asks of me, or rather with what they are asking of themselves. In that space of active and silent listening, a question emerges. It is always appreciative. My experience has shown me, over and over again, that, to open the doors of our inner realms and go into them, we should connect to our strengths, trust and be brave. To do so, it is essential to be appreciative. An appreciative question opens you up gently so that you can see without getting blocked or overwhelmed.

Appreciating, you value, you recognise, you enhance the beauty of the other. Your appreciative presence empowers their self-confidence, opening them up to you and themselves. They open up in order to see and become aware of their self-created monsters which are like paper tigers. With just a match, they can burn them away if so desired, if the courage can be found. They open up to enter silently into themselves and listen. Then we listen together. Together we create a new reality that arises out of feeling ourselves and a generative conversation. Generative, because it generates a different state to the one we had before beginning the conversation. Generative, since it leads us to other spaces where the reality that we create is kind and helps us to go forward.

In coaching I accompany the person to go down the paths that take them within. Perhaps the person is looking to improve a relationship, change jobs or be successful in their endeavour, be it to do with work or personal. On holding a first conversation on what the main topic of the coaching sessions will be, we begin to remove layers of objectives that take them back outside of themselves. We glimpse that the subject to be dealt with covers their life, yes, their work, yes, but above all it covers their heart and mind; in sum, their soul and their relational being, which is fruit of the relationships that they have had and still have.

To accompany you in going more deeply into your soul, if I am not appreciative, I can bring on unnecessary suffering. Forcing it with questions that are more like a blow than a spring-board, I can enable you to open the doors of your inner realms, but I won't have connected you to the passion for the mystery that lies within you; rather to the fears dwelling in the Pandora's box that might open or is already open.

Being appreciative does not mean that I only focus on the positive and on your strengths, but rather that I value your vulnerability as an opportunity, welcome your suffering as a path to go down in order to free you from that which no longer nourishes you, and listen to your doubts and your questions so that they can become the keys which will open your inner realms. Let us look at those paths that lead us there.

# 2. Paths within

We are very taken up with searching outside of ourselves.

We are overstimulated and we depend on being so in order to feel emotions. We live a lot in the mind. We have even left our hearts in order to take up residence in the mind. On making the mind our home, we stay busy by filling it with worries, anxiety, frustrations, upsets and endless thoughts that stir us up and make us act in a different way than we might wish to. Thus, we bury our true heart, the heart of the soul. And in this act of burying we forget. We forget the resources that lie within us. Let us remember them in order to leave behind the meaningless void that so much distraction and noise leaves us in.

Let us remember wisely. One of the keys to transformation is knowing how to forget and how to remember. With remembering we return to our essence, we bring back the memory of our essential being. The capacity to forget and to remember is an extraordinary faculty that we have. If we know how to use it, we will achieve wholeness. Don't forget what you have to remember. Don't remember what you should forget.

To feel complete, it would help you to stop looking outside for what is already within you. You were born with it but you were probably never taught to look inside yourself, and you have spent your life searching on the outside. This brought about misencounters on the path, disappointment and constant dissatisfaction. Dissatisfaction arises from an inner emptiness that you want to fill. But when you are like a bucket with holes in it, it doesn't matter how much water you pour in, the bucket never fills. You run after the desires brought about by this deep dissatisfaction and you stop being present. You are trying to achieve something; when you do, it dissolves in moments like sugar in the mouth. And the dissatisfaction seems impossible to overcome.

To stop being the puppets of our desires, appreciative inquiry proposes that we connect to our essential desire. Knowing what you want helps you to align your energies; that way you manifest the power of a clear intention. Everything we do is propelled by an intention and motivation. It might have as an end the mere fact of satisfying a need, a desire or an addiction, or it might be to achieve a more intangible aim or wish. It is an essential desire because it is aligned with revitalizing and living from your positive core.

### The essence: the positive core

When we accompany people appreciatively, and in appreciative coaching, we awaken the memory, remembering moments that made us vibrate from the depths of our being, and connected us to what in appreciative inquiry we call the positive core. It is about remembering what moves us, discovering it again and feeling it, to thus awaken our deepest dreams and live them. That awakening is a flourishing, an opening to being the best version of oneself and the best version of relationships.

What we long for, what we most seek, lies within us. In our inner space, a core beats that is full of life and of virtues. The positive core is the vital centre of our person; it is what makes us vibrate with enthusiasm and the happiness of living, opening us to our full potential. It contains our essence. The positive core includes our competences, skills, talents and our best achievements and practices, our strengths, unexplored potential and our values. It is a core that grows and flowers; it expands and finds meaning in relationships, in giving oneself and sharing. If one keeps it for oneself, it withers.

Metaphorically, we could say that the positive core is the seed that becomes the sap that gives life to all living systems; it is the blood that circulates round the body of the system of our relationships and interactions. With appreciative inquiry we detect what forms part of the sap, the blood, and nourishes our organs, giving us life and nourishing us.

With the conversations that we hold in coaching, we strengthen the heart that pumps the blood and the organs that clean it. In this way, we revitalize the whole relational system of the person, achieving health and exalting what gives them life. In appreciative coaching sessions, we seek to connect to the positive core, reinforcing it, exalting it and extending it. Even if you don't have coaching, I recommend that you live focused on your essence and on making it flourish, on creating conversations that connect to the essence of other people and the essence of relationship, and on keeping alive the positive core that gives meaning to your relationships.

The positive core is identified in different ways. For example, with appreciative questions we can inquire in order to find it and connect to it. We can also follow a sequence of phases that I will explain further on, but which in essence consist of identifying the positive core through *Defining* what we want to work on and where we want to go towards, and *Discovering* the strengths we have that will support us on the journey; we do this by setting up a dialogue between the person and their relational system. The core is expanded in the *Dreams* phase, when we generate a clear vision, aimed at results relating to the discovered potential that the person wants to manifest more of in their daily life. In the phases of *Design* and *Destiny*, a present is constructed, based on proposals that we design. With these we seek to come close to and live the future that we want, based on the strengths of the positive core of the person and of their relational system, that is, their family, friends, business partners, the necessary people in their lives.

## Live changes building bridges

In order to build a bridge between that which was, that which is, and that which is what we wish it to be, we should take into account the continuity of what we want to keep, what we need to innovate and the transition necessary to cross the bridge and get to where we want. And we cannot do it alone; we need each other.

To cross that bridge, apply the necessary changes and achieve what we want by remaining connected to the positive core, be it in our organisation, our team, family or in ourselves, we should bear three aspects in mind that give us life and keep us in good shape: continuity, innovation and transition. With vision we learn and apply the lessons of the best of the past (continuity), we open ourselves to allow creative ideas to flourish and develop (innovation), and we change our relationship systems and behaviour, holding the necessary conversations that will take us forward towards the desired situation (transition). We will see how to incorporate these three dimensions when I look at the different phases in appreciative coaching, in Part III of this book.

Living means being confronted with often destabilizing changes. Possibly, to prevent those, we will cling on to the intellectual discourse of a mind that needs to understand everything, analyse it, question it, justify it, reason it, conceptualize it, see it and touch it. In the end, your heart stops feeling, blocked by so much analysis and reasoning. These people find it hard to transcend conceptualization. They seek security in concepts. And when change causes them to feel insecure they can fall into the trap of wanting to cling on to any discourse, or else they become cynical and sceptical. They stop being open to other points of view, and in that state it is difficult to innovate and go through the necessary transition.

Other people might find their security and sense of identity not in the mind or intellect, but rather in their habits. They react automatically, almost without thinking or reasoning. Habits rule their lives. The past carries such weight that they live situations and relationships according to the habits acquired along the way. These people are trapped in the prison of their past. Their heart stops enjoying life, as they already live the present in function of the past. Their personal history has such a weight that they stop living in the present, feel afflicted and remain hungry for the oxygen of love. They close into themselves and stop relating freely to themselves and others.

To reside in the heart of being and live life from that central space is to live awakened, and aware of the reality that we are the creators of our thoughts, our beliefs, our reasoning and our habits, which are often culturally and socially conditioned. We can follow them and live accordingly or instead we can challenge them, question them, reinvent them, and reconstruct them in a different way. The important thing is to be aware of our choice. And, therefore, not to complain that "this is what we are like", but rather to take our choice on board and change if we feel like it. There are many perspectives according to which we can live a reality, a relationship and a moment. We can choose to live *mindfully* and *heartfully*, with full awareness and to live fully connected, not only to connect from ideas, from the mind, but also from the heart. To live in full awareness is to feel life. It is to live with the awareness of an awakened heart, a subject that I developed in *La gran liberación, heartfulness y mindfulness* [*The Great Liberation, Heartfulness and Mindfulness*] (2014).

The art of living changes by building bridges requires balance. It is about finding the balance and not going to extremes. About living with feeling, connected to yourself, to God, to your body, to others, to nature and to time, but not losing sight of your dream or the horizons you are walking towards, or want to walk towards. Not giving up on your dream, flowing with the moment, nor getting stuck to your rational plan and no longer flowing.

## What star guides you?

From our consciousness, our being, we can direct our mind, our intellect and our habits. Rooted in our positive core, our life flourishes and, with each step we take, we are inspired and we inspire. So that, instead of being shipwreck survivors drifting depending on the currents, the winds and the waves, we can take the helm of our life and direct it towards the star that we want to guide us. In appreciative coaching we look to find out what that star or constellation is, and how we want to steer our boat, taking into account the other crew members, if there are any, and the conditions of our relational system that cause waves and tides.

Steering our own boat requires us to be aware of our faculties, such as those of the mind to think with, imagine, dream, desire, project and remember; those of the intellect to analyse, reason, discern and decide; and those of the archives of the memory, where we find memories, lived experiences and the images that we have created from what we have lived, our habits and conditionings. Appreciative coaching makes it easier for our mind to think more positively, to connect to the power of our imagination and to visualise the possibility of our dreams. So that we use our faculties, mind, intellect and memory to live in our positive core.

To think positively is not to deny reality, but rather to be capable of seeing problems and having the mental creativity to find solutions without getting obsessed or blinded by something. Positive thoughts strengthen and revitalize the mind. They are usually thoughts based on our values and on appreciating and being grateful for what we are and what we have.

With appreciative coaching, our intellect increases our capacity to analyse and reason from our strengths, to discern from an appreciative position, and to make decisions out of our connection to our positive core. We resort to the archives of our memory in order to remember the positive, what has given us something good, peak experiences we have had, be they of overcoming things, success, or personal power, in order to strengthen the beliefs that help us to flourish as human beings and to banish habits that diminish us. That way, we contribute to creating and strengthening habits that make us into better people and help us to bring the best of ourselves to the world. Making a contribution, we feel useful, a feeling that we need to nurture. Feeling useful makes it worth living, or, in appreciative terms, 'makes it worth the joy of living'.

## Residing in your being

Residing in one's being is to live with full awareness, *heartful*. A heartful person lives with their heart awake. They live with joy and vitality, without anguish or anxiety. They are open and generous. To be heartful is to have a big heart that shares and radiates the best of itself and of that which is outside of itself. It is connected to the supreme force of love, compassion and peace, and it irradiates them. It is an innocent and contented heart. It is clean and honest.

Heartful is a compassionate heart. It is attentive, considerate to the presence of the other; it recognises and sees the other. Each of its words, thoughts and actions can make a miracle happen. A word can open a door to opportunity; a thought can transform a tense atmosphere into one of respect; an action can save a life. A compassionate heart loves out of understanding, forgives and does not stay bitter. It lets go of the past and is grateful to the present. It is strong so as to take on suffering and to live fully the path that heals it. It is a heart that lives in gratitude.

If we live with gratitude and giving thanks, and we also practise meditation, the way is opened up more easily to stop living in the mind, the intellect or our habits, and to moving to residing at the core of being, where the radiant star that is our essence lies, our positive core. This being is like a five-pointed star. Each one of the points represents one of its essential values. They are the values that constitute us as human beings; they are our backbone, the base that gives meaning to our existence.

In the coaching sessions, and also in the meditation ones, I ask people to remember moments of wholeness and to evoke the image of that or those moments. They usually talk to me about the birth of a child or the death of a parent; moments at which the person connected to and felt unconditional love. Or of reaching the top of a mountain; a moment in which the person connected to their personal power and a sense of great perspective. Other times, the image is of a walk in the wood, or being sat on a beach by a tranquil sea at sunset; it is a moment of peace.

An image that also comes when asked to remember a moment of wholeness is when there was a rupture, when the person began on a new and different path, feeling revitalized, free and creative. They connected to their freedom and their personal power which helped them to go through those moments.

With the experiences of so many people, I see time and again that the majority of moments of wholeness are connected to these states and essential values: peace, love, innate wisdom, the authenticity that leads us to freedom, to happiness and to personal power. Let us look at them:

### *Peace*

Peace is serenity and non-violence. It is being quiet with yourself and in harmony. It is being at peace with others, and with your past. If there is some aspect of your past that you haven't come to terms with, you won't be alright in the present moment; the past comes back to you, once, twice or more... because something still needs to be sorted out, redeemed, forgiven, or you haven't reconciled yourself with your past. It is also about being at peace with what you do, and for that it helps to be consistent in your actions. True peace is non-violence in all areas of your life.

### *Love*

When someone lives in their positive core, they live what they are: love. So, in a natural way, you love your neighbour generously, without getting ensnared, without controlling, without needing to possess or be possessed, without the other person losing their freedom nor you yours. With meditation you learn to get this dimension of Love (spelt with a capital) back. You learn to value self, the body, people and what you give to your body. Your body is like the temple of your being, you feed it better, you think better, you are and you live in a more relaxed way. You love what you think. You love what you say. You love what you do. When you live in the positive core, you achieve all this.

### *Innate wisdom*

The heart is wise. The wisdom of the heart guides us so that we can live without doing harm. Its nature is non-violent. We have such potential for love and wisdom in the heart of our being that we can heal the planet. For this we should awaken the potential of our heart.

The awakened heart intuits, feels and understands the other. It sees the essential even if it is invisible to the eyes. It doesn't need logical reasoning or justifications. It knows what it is. The voice of the heartful conscience is intuition.

Our intuition guides us. When you connect to your intuition, you don't fail. You, your being, are wise. How many times do we have the intuition to do something but our logic, our mind, our beliefs, say to us: "No, no, not that way, this way." Afterwards you think: "I should have followed my intuition." We don't trust in this intuition because there is a mixture of desires, fears, opinions and beliefs that interfere.

The intuition is the faculty of an awakened conscience. With it, you are aware of what is happening inside and outside and you have a global perspective. Intuition gives us direct access, without passing through the rational, to information that we are not normally aware of. It is the capacity that we have to know something without a logical basis. You know something without knowing how you know it; you intuit it and you are right. Intuition helps you to stay on track in moments of uncertainty. It connects you to your inner compass, to the star that guides you.

## *Authenticity*

It could also be called purity, sincerity, honesty, or transparency. Today we see an abundance of corruption, lies, deceit, because we have strayed from the heart of being and we live on the edges: as temporary and fleeting characters, identities, roles and labels.

In the authenticity of being, one is freed of false identities, of characters that are not really us. It is a freedom that leads us to be happy. The basis of happiness is freedom. Living the authenticity of the positive core, you feel the true wholeness of the self: a wholeness that does not come from the outside in, but rather emerges and is transmitted from the inside out. In one's authentic state, one lacks nothing that is essential.

## *Personal power*

When we are connected to our inner roots, we live the conviction that we can. We can be what we are and we can be alright. "There is nothing as indestructible as a convinced man. No obstacle is insurmountable when there is true faith."[3]

We are singular. Let us not be afraid of shining, of being unique and being different. Our personal singularity is the gift that we can bring to the world and to our relationships. We are enriched by giving of ourselves and sharing. Appreciative coaching honours the singularity of each person, their exceptionality and the essential and differential elements that they bring to the process. Each person is special, different and unique. The singular one is original, noticeable, surprising, excellent, extraordinary, strange, distinct, unusual, atypical, different, exceptional and mysterious. Our singularity is heightened on sharing it as we are social beings and we need each other in order to be and fulfil the potential of what we are, to live together and share, to flourish.

With appreciative inquiry we discover the singularity of each person and we encourage and awaken it; in this way all the talent and personal capacity flourish. If you also meditate, meditation helps you to listen to the voice that tunes in with your being. Your being is originally peaceful, authentic, loving, wise and strong because it is rooted in your essence. By meditating you reach the heart of the self, the temple of the self that has not been contaminated by fears, selfishness, greed, negativity, the useless and superfluous. You connect to the positive core that revitalizes you and gives you strength to live what is authentic, that resides in you and is you.

# 3. In search of liberation

In order to live your essence, in your positive core, which consists in what I have explained in chapter 2, you need to allow yourself to do so and free yourself of fears, limiting beliefs and feelings of guilt and bitterness. The person whose spirit is freed of all these things controls their mind, directs their thought and keeps their attention focused. Their heart is at peace, and radiates positive energy and love. Their action is aligned with their values, decisions and will. Their being lives together and flows with others.

Our creative capacity to choose what we think and what we feel at each moment, and how we respond to each situation, is our strength and our freedom. However, our beliefs limit us, our past conditions us, and our fears prevent us from living out our deepest dreams. If we want to live free from our self-limiting conditionings, we have to know ourselves better, question our beliefs, clean out the storeroom of memories that keep us anchored in the past, and overcome our fears, which hold us back and block our immense creative energy. To accompany each other in living with this spirit of freedom, we can ask each other – Are you sure? Every time someone makes a convinced statement, we can make them question their convictions so that they open up to bringing in other perspectives.

In the following chapters, I will explain how the appreciative perspective in accompanying people and appreciative coaching contribute to the process of liberation. Here, now, I am explaining what we can achieve. In Part III of the book, I share with you how to achieve it and what principles and stages we can follow.

To flourish together, it is important to understand the habits that we have created which influence, condition and tie us down. We were not born with them; we created them as we went along.

Some are habits that deprive us of our personal freedom; others limit our potential. It might even be that these habits come to generate a slavery or addiction on an emotional and mental level. Some habits have been cultivated in the midst of relationships that, in the end, became dependent and toxic.

Freedom consists, amongst other things, of being capable of thinking, feeling and expressing our thoughts and feelings, without being conditioned by external factors or the negative tendencies of our personality, and without causing pain. Yes, we should take circumstantial factors and relationships into account, time and place, but we should not act as victims of all of it; rather, it would be healthier to take care of others and ourselves. The person who acts like a victim feels that they cannot be at the helm of their life because their relationships are controlling them and circumstances overwhelm and confuse them. At the least, if we feel conditioned, let us be aware of it and of the possibility of choosing other perspectives. And, depending on the conditions, of choosing the best to care for ourselves and others.

It is about being capable of living in positive emotions, in the feelings that exalt our life, and in opening up assertively the conversations that matter to us and that lead us forward. It is to be able to go through negative emotions without drowning in them.

In order to live with greater freedom, let us learn to ask ourselves the powerful questions that will act as keys that open doors for us. This will help us to broaden our vision and be more aware. Asking ourselves the right questions helps us to receive the necessary answers. Even if we have the answer in front of us, if we haven't asked the question we will not receive or perceive the answer. If we can formulate the question, we will see that the answer is at the threshold of our door.

To formulate the question that will open us up and free us, we should understand the context, and the fact that we live by basing ourselves on a series of beliefs that make up our view of life, our attitudes, our decisions and our behaviour. These beliefs are sociological, psychological, cultural, political, religious and spiritual. They are beliefs about what is good and what is bad; about good and evil; about what success is and what failure is. And so on to an endless list of beliefs that make up our conditionings and the *status quo* in which we live. With the appreciative principles we open ourselves to other points of view and we learn to question appreciatively. If we didn't do this, we would bring about a defensive attitude and push people to stick even more to their own convictions.

What is it that leads you to be convinced of something? Are you sure? Can beliefs free us? Or, in sum, do we have to transcend certain beliefs? In the experience of contemplative silence we transcend everything, including our individualistic and dual self. We enter into the dimension of pure clarity. As Pablo d'Ors (2012) expresses well: "When you no longer have nor are anything, you are finally free. You are the inner territory itself; not only are you in your homeland, you are your homeland." In this pilgrimage towards your homeland, the destiny of freedom is not far away or outside; it is a second and a millimetre away. It is you and it is in you.

Let us look at another important aspect in the journey towards our inner self and in the longing for freedom. It is the suffering that we store inside ourselves and our relationships. To what extent do we confuse the escape mechanisms of suffering with freeing ourselves of it? We will go deeper into the understanding of suffering in our lives and relationships in the next chapter.

# 4. Going through suffering and vulnerability

One can put up resistance to living a return to oneself, given that, as Thich Nhat Hanh states (1997), "The majority of people are afraid of returning to themselves, because they fear facing the pain that is within them."

When you have a family member, a loved one or friend suffering, you can accept their suffering, but if you want to help them to be freed from it, focus on their desire for growth and in what they long for. You can ask them questions that accompany them in seeing their light, that change the direction of where they are looking and their thinking; instead of focusing on the shadow, let them look at the light and be able to feel grateful.

In appreciative coaching we recognise the suffering and pain that the other feels, also understanding their desire for growth and development, and focusing on this latter. The appreciative coach does not deny the appearance of suffering or the expression of vulnerability in the coaching sessions. Rather, when they appear, the coach turns into the *thinking partner* (chapter 21): they uphold the field of the client by asking them some question that allows them to see where to find their own light. They don't delve into the causes of the suffering, they don't indulge in investigating the whys and hows of the apparition of the suffering. They don't take the client into greater depths of suffering, but rather permit them to observe themselves and change their perspective, change the angle they position themselves from, to see and incorporate other points of view. It is a question of seeing what the suffering makes possible, and of being aware of what it is offering them – what is it saying to them? It is about contributing to the recovery of their inner power so as not to remain emotionally devastated and mentally anguished.

It is not only as coaches, but also as friends that we can be thinking partners for each other. As a thinking partner I can contribute to the person before me being able to listen to themselves. To them being aware that, if they don't listen to what the suffering is telling them, a moment comes when an inner split opens up. We have fled from our own inner voice that wishes to communicate something to us. In taking on the suffering and making it ours, we will feel that it is speaking to us. Suffering indicates the possibility of a latent change, a transformation that can lead to greater depth. When we find the meaning of our suffering, it is transformed.

When we are motivated towards something, we go through the difficulties that present themselves in order to achieve it. Motivation helps us to go forward. In appreciative coaching we set our sights on images of the future that attract us and awaken motivation and enthusiasm. As we are motivated, it is easier for us to face suffering and to be able to go through it, looking at it with an appreciative point of view and a perspective of gratitude.

"Suffering indicates to us that something new is being born. If we go backwards, the very thing calling us to be transformed gets infected. If we take it on board and we go through it, the old falls away and the new is born. It becomes necessary to flow with uncertainty, since one doesn't know what will happen after letting go of the outer covering. You don't know what is waiting for you after that change, and this uncertainty can cause you to have a lack of inner strength. However, letting go of that which when we release it frees us, strengthens us and makes us free."

"Sometimes as a friend, or if it is the case, coach, the only thing I have to do is listen. I realise that the mere fact of sharing the difficulty, of giving it a name and expressing it, lightens the burden of the person speaking to me. If they identify it, they name it, they listen to it and we look at it in the eye, we make it human. What happens sometimes is that the shame or fear of what people will think on seeing our vulnerability or weakness, or that they will label us a failure, makes it difficult for us to share our suffering." Looked at appreciatively and in constructive conversation, that fear is dissipated.

"We should learn to accompany in suffering without judging the other. A loving look that receives that pain and does not judge when someone opens themselves to be listened to and to share helps them to express themselves in order to let go of the suffering accumulated inside us. And the more we think that we would be judged, or seen in a bad light, the more we discover the look of tenderness and understanding of the other who is close to us, and this is profoundly freeing. Having somewhere to express and manifest it unloads a lot of the burden that one might feel. Being seen humanises us and allows us to go forward." [4] Let us widen our perspectives.

# 5. Broadening perspectives

Living appreciative inquiry, the appreciative principles and working as an appreciative coach has opened me, and continues to open me every day, to new perspectives, extending my vision and my capacity to receive what I see. It makes me question my own ideas and beliefs. As I understand and experience social constructionism more (page 64), I learn to include different perspectives. This helps me to take decisions in a more inclusive and aware way, recognising and appreciating the existence of the other and their different perspectives.

We suffer because we stay stuck in points of view, perspectives and habits that we refuse to modify. "We only suffer because we think things should be otherwise. As soon as we abandon this idea, we stop suffering. As soon as we stop imposing our own ideas on to reality, reality stops presenting itself as adverse or prone and begins to show itself as it is, without that value pattern that prevents us from reaching it. The path of meditation is therefore that of detachment, that of the rupture of mental frameworks or prejudices: it is a process of undressing to the point that we find out that we are much better naked."[5]

In the sessions of accompaniment, I establish other possible ways of looking that might help us to break down rusty mental frameworks and, gently, with grace, with appreciation, we go towards the space of the positive core, the vital centre of our person, that which makes us vibrate with enthusiasm and the joy of living and opens us up to our full potential.

In order to widen your vision you can do an observation exercise in silence: Relax. Breathe deeply. Think: "I am not this situation. I separate from it. I quieten my mind. I think: nothing is permanent. Everything will pass."

Develop that capacity to free yourself from the influences that diminish you and put out your flame; those that reduce your ability to love, to shine, to feel free, to be at peace. Those influences come from the outside, and also from your past and your habits.

It becomes necessary to include the practice of silence, patience, and the capacity for reflection, in order not to react instinctively, responding to fear and insecurity out of fright or anger, but rather responding out of your values, trust, love, respect, listening, tolerance, creativity and inner strength.

Try to clean out the storerooms of your mind, the archives inside your being, so that no habit leads you to react with bitterness, jealousy, hate and fear. To reach that state of wholeness in which there is a balance between the mind and the heart, feel how you respond in accordance with your values, your positive core. To achieve it, you should overcome the feelings that block that experience, strengthen your self-esteem, clarity, self-command and personal sovereignty, and develop the powers that will help you to face problems and transcend influences.

Let us explore these aspects:

- To feel responding to your values is to live your essence and be connected to your roots. Let the sap of your essence flow through all your being and feed into your life, keeping you energetic and healthy. It is to live your positive core.
- Overcoming the feelings that block the experience of wholeness requires you to explore what diminishes your presence: mental confusion, negative thoughts, blaming yourself, worries, projections, and comparing yourself. See page 166.
- To extend and maintain clarity, it will help you to be aware and realise where you come from, where you are, where you are going and what is happening in the here and now.
- To achieve personal sovereignty means to be in charge of

> yourself. Living in full awareness will help you to get back your inner power in order to deal with problems and overcome debilitating influences.

In these pages, it is my desire to transmit the importance of broadening perspectives and the multiple routes that are possible in order to achieve this. The appreciative perspective transforms. Let us look at the dimensions of the value of appreciating.

# 6. Appreciating[6]

Perhaps you are surprised by the emphasis on the use of the word "appreciative". We are going to look at the value offered by appreciation. Let's begin with your own experience.

Remember a moment in which you were appreciated; a moment when you felt that others valued you. Perhaps they recognised you for what you were doing, for what you were, or what you were sharing. You can remember it now and, when the memory arises, reflect upon:

How you felt?
What happened?
What effect it had on you?

Stop reading these pages for a while and remember that moment. If several come to mind, remember one in particular. Write it down.

Remember what you felt when you were appreciated. How did it help you?

We seek to be seen and to be recognised. Our beings are often conditioned according to how others see us and how their opinions influence us. When we appreciate the other, we see them, we recognise them and we value them.

To appreciate is:

- To value.
- The act of recognising the best in people and in the world that surrounds us.
- To affirm the strengths of the past and present, successes and potential.

- To perceive the things that give life, health, vitality and excellence to living systems.
- To increase the value of something.
- To welcome and receive, esteem, honour, respect, recognise, increase the value, be grateful for, and affirm.

When we appreciate, we move forward: our mind opens up to receive, to recognise new data and to learn. Appreciating, we feel surprise and curiosity. When we appreciate, we discover the best of 'what is' and we open ourselves to see 'what could be'. Appreciating with passionate and absorbing effort, in which we invest emotional and cognitive energy, helps us to generate a positive image of the future that we desire. In appreciating, new values emerge.

The capacity to appreciate arises out of a mental state and from an attitude that shows itself through the skill of perceiving what is valuable and meaningful about oneself, the other and the world. An appreciative attitude increases people's capacity to be generative and influence others, and with this, their ability to generate freeing changes is multiplied. Developing appreciative skills helps us to create and increase our happiness and well-being. "Happiness is a mental state, a way of perceiving ourselves and of conceiving of ourselves and the world around us," states Sonja Lyubomirsky.[7]

When we appreciate ourselves, we strengthen our self-esteem. On discovering and valuing the best of what we have, we provide ourselves with resources with which to deal with life. When this discovery is sincere, we feel an emotional connection to our strengths and capacities. Positive emotions awaken in us – respect for oneself, happiness, hope and inspiration, amongst others. With these positive emotions we open ourselves to learning. Positive emotions open us, negatives ones close us. Thanks to self-confidence, we dare to take on risks. When we appreciate that what we do is important and can make a difference in our lives and in the world, we feel strengthened and we do it better.

When appreciating the other becomes a habit and a vital attitude, we increase the quality of our relationships and we contribute to bringing out the best in people. Some disciplines base their results on appreciating others and on generating expectations for the achievement of surprising results. For example, some methodologies have worked out theories based on what is known as the Pygmalion effect to denominate the actions that we undertake due to the expectations that others have of us. We are sensitive to what our significant others expect of us. The expectations of others can change our levels of effort, and have an influence on the profound concept that we have of ourselves.

To practise the appreciative perspective with others is to focus on the talents, strengths and values of the person, and see the best in them. It is not to put on to the other what we would like them to have; it is to practise appreciative intelligence. It is to see the oak tree in the acorn, as I explained in the introduction.

Increasing our appreciative capacities allows us to create positive images of the future. The emotions awakened by our personal interpretation of images lead us to create an optimistic or pessimistic future in our mind. "Positive emotions arise as we interpret events and ideas as they develop; it depends on whether we give ourselves a moment to find the good, and, once found, let it flow," says Barbara Fredrickson (2011). If we take the necessary time and we have the intention of maintaining an attitude of appreciation, positive emotions will flourish and open the way for us to live out our full potential.

# 7. Living to your full potential

I find myself on the sofa listening to Mercedes, then to Javier, also to Pedro, to Florián and to Silvia, and to other people that have passed through my consulting room. All of them share one affliction: they feel that they cannot develop their true potential in their work, that they don't have the opportunity to grow with their life partner either, and they are looking for a way out for that potent seed that lies inside them and wants to grow until it flourishes. If their creativity remains shut away, the person suffocates.

The ideal for me is to live to my full potential, flourishing together with others. To be more creative. To construct my best present, respecting the environment. To construct our best present taking each other into account, seeing and recognising each other. To feel each day with joy and gratitude. To broaden my mind and the power of the imagination, and widen my heart and the power to love. All this with the intention of building a more habitable world together with others, in which each one might live to their full potential.

What do you need to live the intensity of the instant, to savour the beauty of this moment, to connect to your full potential and open it up so that it can show itself? Some of the necessary fundamental elements in order to develop your full potential are: connection to your essence, your positive core; concentration; mental preparedness; trust; positive images; commitment, courage and continuous learning. Let us look at them in brief:

### *Connection to your positive core*

In chapter 2, "Paths within", I looked at the importance of finding our essential being and connecting to our positive core. On living connected to our essence, we flourish and contribute to the flourishing of others. See page 11.

### *Concentration*

Concentrating helps you to control distractions until they are dissipated. It is the state in which the mind focuses on an object, on a thing, a word, an image, an idea. The mind wanders for lack of mental discipline, lack of clarity and will to achieve it or lack of vision and passion for what one wants. Sometimes it is a matter of putting limits to our distractions and interruptions. It might help us to develop our capacity to concentrate if we create positive thoughts connected to what motivates us and what we want, and use them as affirmations to strengthen the concentration. We can create a list of thoughts that are like keys to be used to open the flow of inner positivity. For example: I can; I don't let myself be influenced; I am love; everything was as it had to be, I accept it and I let it go.

Meditation is a fundamental practice with which to develop concentration and be capable of thinking what we want to think, avoiding repetitive, useless or negative thoughts. Meditating helps you to silence the unnecessary voices, and thus develop the capacity to be centred and concentrate.

If we focus on something we like, it is easier to concentrate. Experience shows us that we need discipline in order to achieve what we want and reach where we long to get to. An athlete needs discipline to stay fit and thus reach the goals they establish for themselves. A team must train with discipline in order to play with excellence on the day of the match. When someone loves their purpose and their goals, they enjoy the practice and undertake the discipline naturally. First, we need to have a clear vision of what we want and what motivates us. The motivation to satisfy the objectives that we have set out for ourselves will help us to incorporate discipline as a necessary part of the process, and the concentration will come then in a natural way.

Learning to discipline your mind in order to control your

thoughts will allow you to be in charge of them and will enable you to create healthy attitudes. You will take on board the responsibility of creating your destiny with will and perseverance instead of feeling yourself to be a victim, and complaining of being trapped in a situation that makes you unhappy. You can substitute the habit of complaining for the habit of being grateful. To substitute one habit for another you need will and discipline. These will help you to keep your focus and concentration on what you want.

What usually happens when we set out to incorporate a practice, transform a habit, or make an effort to achieve an objective, is that a self-boycott appears. One boycotts one's own aims. Discipline helps us to overcome our saboteur and the inner critic that sabotages our intentions. They are the doubts and fears that hold us back and block us. With clarity and will we can overcome them and thus achieve our aim. To achieve it we need mental preparedness.

### *Mental availability*

Learning to release, let go and detach oneself, one opens up a space in the mind and being. The mind, on no longer being oversaturated with information and unnecessary thoughts, has space and can be available. It is a question of keeping an open attitude. Being curious and feeling curiosity. With appreciative principles I accompany people in opening themselves, and thus their mind starts to leave their own traps. They start opening themselves to a more appreciative state that allows them to incorporate new data and let go of the old data that is no longer of use to them. If they resist, there is no opening. In accepting, you can let go and you are more ready for your inner strength to emerge.

Being available requires serenity. Serenity is a natural state of being. It is only possible to be serene when we stop wanting to control situations and people, when we accept uncertainty and impermanence as natural states of the constant change that living implies, and when we are at peace with our acts.

Within yourself, you will find serenity. If you flee from yourself, you will not learn to manage your thoughts or to transcend your noise. If you take inside you one of the issues you are trying to deal with, you will not find yourself, because that issue will take up too much space, covering up the essential. You will remain connected to that issue and the people involved in it.

With a calmed mind and a serene heart, we know how to pick up on and understand the signals that situations are giving to us, and we also pick up on the signals of the time, of the moment that we are living in. We are more available.

### *Trust*

Trust is a basic willingness to flow in life and deal with its uncertainties and complexities successfully on an emotional level. Without trust there is no hope, freedom, tolerance or the possibility of learning from one's errors, meaning that it is difficult to build one's self-esteem and build healthy relationships.

Hellenic wisdom denominated *empistosini*, or 'believe in', to the term trust. The word *confide* derives from the Latin, and, in fact, could be translated as 'sin fiducia' or 'item given by the one who contracts as security against the fulfilment of their obligation'. Without shared faith, we cannot have projects in cooperation. As relational beings, con-fidence (trust) is basic in order to go forward in the expression of our full potential.

The free decision to trust can be situated on a scale that ranges from deep trust to active mistrust. Deep trust generates the creation of solid and stable human bonds; it is the main source of commitment and fidelity in the interpersonal relationship. Without trust there is no free commitment. Trust acts as a 'sticking glue' in the relationships between people, groups, organisations and societies. Without trust, bonds get broken and there is disintegration, and interpersonal, organisational and social fragmentation.

One thing is the trust or belief in oneself and self-confidence; another, trust in others, in the future of humanity, in our political leaders, and in the company project that one might be participating in (hetero-confidence); the trust of others towards us, or trustworthiness is another. When we trust, and are in an environment of trust, it is easier for us to live our full potential.

We generate trust when we show ourselves to have integrity; we want the good of the other, we demonstrate the ability to meet their needs, we are appreciative, adopt a positive emotional tone and maintain good self-esteem. Both people and social systems are more disposed towards trust if they possess inner security, if they have good self-esteem and self-confidence, if they are within themselves in an empowered way.

We tend to trust in others (hetero-confidence) and to love them in the measure that we trust in ourselves and have high self-esteem. It is easier to trust in someone who has good self-esteem.

We will look at the trust in the relationship that is established between the coach and the client on page 141.

## *Positive images*

> Reality is conditioned, it is reconstructed and, often, it is created through our anticipatory images. Change begins in the images that we have of the future.
> – David Cooperrider (2008)

The images that attract and inspire us give us strength to change structures and improve the economy. The changes that are substantial and sustained over time do not begin in the economy or in structures, but rather in the images we maintain. These push us to change or to stay stuck and unable to move forward. Change is deeper to the extent that we are capable of creating new images of the future that are attractive and that stimulate us to be creative. Positive images have an influence on personal, relational, political, social, cultural, communal and organisational change. They turn into guiding images that attract us towards constructing the future we long for.

In the years of my experience in sessions accompanying people, I have realised how images mobilise their inner world. When the image that we have changes for one that is more positive and attractive, our vision changes, our attitude is modified and our vital state improves. When we are stuck in the images of the past, especially in those based on what didn't work, what betrayed us or deceived us, change is more difficult or doesn't happen because, on bringing those images to the present, we remain blocked. We feel anger, fear or sadness, and we find it hard to move forward.

If you go out into the world in the morning with your mind full of pessimistic images of what the day will bring, your attitude will be sad or resigned. If, on the other hand, you go out into the day with images that inspire you, your attitude will be more proactive and you will go through your day in better conditions.

Focusing on what works, and on what we most want, helps us to find positive images of our experiences. It is from that positive emotional space that we can perceive the future that we want. Keeping it on our horizon, our inner potential flowers and leads us towards what we want to reach.

We will see more on the power of positive images when I look at the anticipatory principle (page 89) and the dreams phase (page 118).

In any case, even if we trust and have images that attract us towards a future that we want in the present, without commitment, it will be difficult to achieve. Let us look at the value of commitment.

### *Commitment and courage*

Commitment unleashes power and invites the universe to help. Without commitment we do not move forward. Without commitment we do not grow. I realise that many people set out to do things that they do not do because they do not commit themselves to them. Our will has weakened. We are the puppets of our desires and of circumstances, and our determination has stayed dormant or is hanging from a thread.

With difficulty will you be able to take your highest longings to your daily life if you don't act with commitment. You need a level of commitment that is passionate and sincere, that helps you to overcome the weaknesses and events and unforeseen things that place themselves in your way. With commitment you will see how your energies flow. You have to propose it to yourself, you must want to, decide to, have the willpower and do it. Now. Commit yourself and act. Dare to commit yourself. Commit yourself in a decided way to the practice of new attitudes, thoughts and actions. Cultivate your wholeness, you deserve it. Dare to free yourself of what you don't need any more, of what isn't yours, of what has already gone.

Goethe described the results of commitment thus:

> Until one commits oneself, the doubt is there, the possibility of going back, always without benefit. With regards to all acts of initiative (and of creation), there is an elemental truth, the ignorance of which kills an endless number of ideas, as well as splendid plans: that at the moment that one truly commits oneself, Providence also acts. To help someone, all kinds of things occur that, without having taken the decision to commit, would never happen. A whole series of events are set in motion out of the decision, bringing about, in one's favour, all kinds of unforeseen incidents, encounters and material help that no one would ever have dreamed might have happened. Anything that you can dream that you can do,

begin to do it. Daring carries with it genius, power and magic. Start now!

Committing yourself implies connecting to your dreams. Keeping them in your vision. Don't lose sight of the horizon or the aim. Clarify your goals. Create the best in yourself, offer the best of yourself, be your best version and don't feed the other versions (the mediocre ones, the atrophied ones, the infantile, the complicated ones). If your horizon fades away and you feel confused, delve into yourself. Enter into silence. Wait. Don't lose yourself in an impulse. Listen.

Feel curiosity for everything that happens inside you and for everything around you, not taking at face value the automatic answers that your ego character gives to your questions. Always look for your inner truth and what is authentic on the outside, so as not to get carried away by mirages.

You can ask yourself:

What do I want for myself?
Why and for what do I exist?
What does life ask of me?
What is it offering me to do?
What do I do? Or what am I doing? What do I do it for?
What do I pay attention to? What am I focusing on? Carried away by my attention, am I present or absent?

Being in the present in this moment you reinforce your essence and the essential. Which deserves joy (not sorrow!). On observing, you can redirect your attention.

To develop our full potential we should be alert and aware of not believing that we have reached our goal when we are perhaps only halfway. Mariana Caplan explains this well in her book *Halfway Up the Mountain* (1999).

### *Continuous learning*

We never know enough, although paradoxically everything that we need to know to be happy and to be fine resides within us, and reveals itself and flowers in our relational spaces. Appreciative inquiry does not offer us a linear process that begins and ends, but rather a spiral that rises and makes us flourish more and better each day. As we inquire, we discover that there is more to inquire about, to learn and to design. This opening keeps us young and mentally agile.

Appreciative coaching activates positive emotions such as happiness and enjoyment. People feel good. This reinforces hope. When positive emotions awaken, this improves cognitive functioning, access to the information of the memory and the integration of information. All this stimulates the parasympathetic nervous system, which in turn stimulates the liberation of various endocrine glands in the blood associated with physiological, psychological and social benefits for the human being. These effects have been studied by Barbara Fredrickson, Richard Boyatzis, and Barsade and Gibson, amongst others. Boyatzis states that on stimulating the parasympathetic nervous system, the immune response is better and there is even a reversing of some of the damage caused by chronic stress. All this facilitates learning and the incorporation of new data. Fredrickson says that, on living positive emotions on a scale of 4-1, that is, 4 positive for 1 negative, our mental capacity for learning is increased.

# 8. Language of abundance

The language of abundance is the one that in its narratives uses words focused on what one has and what one wants. It implies using inspiring and affirmative words instead of narrating from what is lacking and what does not work. A change in discourse is needed, given that, as Peter Senge states: "Often we spend so much time resolving problems along the way that we only have a minimal, even inexact, idea of what is really important for us." We use a language of problem solving, focusing on what is not going well and doesn't work, on what needs to be fixed. Our conversations and efforts are centred on solving what isn't going well, instead of creating what we wish for and building the best future.

The majority of interventions, consultants and accompaniments, whose objective it is to make changes in an organisation or for a person to change their present situation, have approaches that begin by talking about the problem that needs to be resolved; they analyse what didn't work and, often, they look for the person who is to blame or responsible for the situation. Appreciative inquiry goes in another direction; it asks when people and the organisation were in their best, at a peak moment and what it was that gave life to the system, leading us to a search for sources of imagination, creativity and energy. In the narration promoted by appreciative inquiry, we use a language of abundance.

That is, in the traditional practice of problem resolution, consultants and mediators:

- Feel the need.
- Identify the problem or problems.
- Analyse them.
- Look for the causes.

- Analyse the possible solutions.
- Propose an action plan.
- And finally, a 'treatment' is put into action.

In this process a language of lack and deficit is used. That is, we speak about what is lacking, what is not working and what the difficulties are.

However, in the practice of appreciative inquiry, the focus is inspiring and evokes images of the desired future:

- Appreciate: what is it that gives us life?
- Imagine: how could it be?
- Dialogue: how should it be?
- Innovate: how will it be?

To live appreciating, imagining, dialoguing and innovating makes us feel that the inquiry *is* change and that, with it, we discover the positive core of a person, a team and an organisation. To live appreciative inquiry is to live a change in language.

Sometimes, we find people who want to talk about what they don't want or don't like in their organisation. They are fed up and about to explode. Their language is of deficit. During the appreciative inquiry, it is not a question of avoiding these subjects, especially if they are accompanied by an emotional burden. Not to offer them the possibility of talking about this will disconnect those people and put them into an absent state; they will not participate happily. It is necessary to be careful when creating the space to inquire into feelings of hurt, of injustice, anger, unhappiness or despair.

When we participate in a conversation in which there are upset, wounded or angry feelings, let us choose the questions we ask at that moment with care. We might lean on the possibility of talking about their aspirations and of creating an image of what they want. For example, instead of asking what it is they don't like, we can ask what they think is needed, what it is that they most want, what image they have of how their environment should be, and their ideal future. These kinds of questions have a greater generative potential, as they lead people to look for what attracts them, and to detach from what frustrates and angers them.

We need positive visions that inspire and mobilise us. We can no longer sustain the old paradigm, which seeks and analyses what doesn't work, and tries to put sticking plaster over it. We need to create something new out of our imagination, intuition and intention, which includes the global well-being and not just that of a few. And we should do it including the voice of everyone. That is why, in appreciative coaching, we include the system of the people we are accompanying. We understand the system as their relational circle and environment. When one piece changes, it affects everything around it. In what way will their change bring benefits to their relationships? What should they take into account for their change to have a positive influence? What steps should they take and what conversations should they have in order to feel accompanied by the people around them who are important to them?

When we talk about what we want and about our dreams, we go from the discourse based on deficit to a discourse based on strengths. Achieving this is not easy because we have baggage and habits that have led us for a long time to focus on what is lacking. We get stuck in what we don't like and it is difficult for us to change the conversation. I often find that on asking: "What do you want?" the person starts answering and within a minute goes back to the difficulties and what doesn't work. Our language is more about deficit than abundance. The change of discourse requires a change of language. We need to be alert and attentive to the baggage that we carry. And reformulate the question: "I am aware that there are difficulties. Now leave them to the side for a moment and allow yourself to imagine how your life would be if you achieved your ideal. What would be happening? How would you feel? What would you achieve?"

Through our conversations we create our present and our future. What do we talk about? How inspiring are our conversations? What words do we use that allow us to create and imagine better presents and futures? To what point is our perception tainted by the conversations that we hold?

To bring about a change of discourse in conversations the following attitudes and proposals will help you:

- Appreciate. On appreciating you open yourself and you open others. On opening new possibilities, new words and images emerge.
- Value the best of what is.
- Visualise what could be.
- Accompany others in order to see and dream what could be.
- Encourage dialogue.
- Open doors to the design of what should be.
- Facilitate the creative attitude of innovation.
- Support that which will be.
- Ask questions with positive and appreciative assumptions.
- Feel comfortable in the space of 'not knowing' and facilitate the expression of individual and collective knowledge.

With appreciative coaching we see that it is not only a question of living to your full potential on your own, but rather of doing it together with others and of flourishing together. This is based on social constructionism. Let us find out what this is and how to apply it in Part II of this book.

# Part II

# Flourishing together

Love is rather dangerous, it brings with it the only revolution that gives complete happiness.[8]
– Krishnamurti

# 9. Flourishing

When a human being flourishes, they express the best of themselves. They are creative, intuitive and life-giving. They promote innovation and renewal from the centre of their being and connect to others with happiness and positivity. Barbara Fredrickson defines flourishing as feeling oneself to be fully alive, a creative and resilient being (capable of overcoming adversity), and feeling that we are growing and having a positive impact on our environment.

For Martin Seligman, the objective of positive psychology is flourishing, which is based on the five pillars of his theory of well-being. In the theory of well-being, analysing the PERMA model, Seligman invites us to think about what we have to do to prosper and be happy, and he represents the five essential elements that should be in place in order to experience ongoing well-being:

- Positive emotions: Well-being is experienced through positive emotions.
- Engagement: Being engaged with something allows us to experience motivation and well-being.
- Relationships: Relationships are important for our well-being. The people who have a positive relationship with others are happier than those who do not.
- Meaning: Meaning comes from serving a cause that is bigger than ourselves. If it is a cause that helps humanity, this gives meaning to our lives and brings us well-being.
- Accomplishment: Accomplishment is important insofar as it contributes to our capacity to prosper.

To cultivate positive emotions we focus on what works and we make it grow, and we centre on what is life-giving. It is also necessary to manage suffering so that it is not devastating (see chapter 4) and, finally, not to allow certain toxic people or relationships to pollute our inner spaces. I have relationships with people together with whom I have created a sacred space, of complete friendship and trust. But a third person appears on the scene who talks badly of one and of another, and, if I am not careful, their negative perspective can pollute those sacred spaces. When this happens to you, you start to imagine things and to think badly; the seed of mistrust may be sown. You have opened the door to negativity and unease. In those cases, pay attention so as not to feed the negative assumptions. For me, what works is the agreement of Miguel Ruiz, in which he advises:

> Don't make assumptions or draw conclusions from everything in a precipitative way. If you do that, you believe that what you suppose is true and you create a reality about it. It is not always positive nor guided by love. Have the courage to ask, clarify, and express what you want. Communicate with others as clearly as you can in order to avoid misunderstandings, sadness and other dramas. With just this agreement you can completely transform your life.[9]

When assumptions take root in our being, we blame, we complain and we feel anger, we create dramas in relationships and we lose our handle on situations. Our energy and mental clarity are reduced, and we end up as victims of external factors and of fear, anger and sadness. It is difficult for us to stop being victims when we keep on with habits of clinging, getting too attached and depending. With them, our heart loses vitality and our capacity to flourish remains cut off. The pressure that these emotional states generate and the absence of freedom cause us suffering and nurture our feelings of victimhood. We are so accustomed to these forms of suffering that we come to believe they are natural. It is possible to stop going through these emotional upsets when we recover our inner power.

The capacity to decide what we think and feel at each moment, the possibility of choosing our attitude and how to respond in each situation is our strength and our freedom. We can choose to think and feel in such a way as to flourish and stay open. We have the possibility of using our immense creative power in different spheres of life. However, our beliefs and partial points of view limit us, the past conditions us, and fears prevent us from living out our dearest dreams. When this happens, instead of flourishing in shared living, we get bogged down and we enter into conflict. Then we prefer to be and live alone. We run from conflict and from relational complications. We want peace. And when we feel trapped in relationships that suffocate us, peace disappears, giving way to anguish. We feel misunderstood, and flooded with worries. At other times it seems as if we should submit ourselves to the desires of others in order to please them. All this oppresses us. On feeling threatened by the presence of the other, we end up renouncing our individual integrity, too influenced by others and society. We look for security and we stop being ourselves, taking on a personality that follows cultural and social models, not aligned with ourselves.

Then, instead of establishing positive relationships, as Seligman advises in his PERMA model, our relationships are the source of unhappiness. Our inner misalignment makes it difficult for us to establish healthy relationships. All this pushes us to escape to an arid aloneness or to take refuge in a toxic kind of shared living. Even though we are with someone else, we feel alone and disconnected.

## Being alone despite the presence of another

Juana is afraid of being alone. She always tries to please and do the right thing. She usually agrees with everyone else in order not to risk being rejected. That way she feels accepted and that she belongs to the group. She renounces herself out of fear of rejection and ending up on her own. She gives up her power to others and turns into a puppet who allows herself to be moulded according to what others want of her. She is always at the beck and call of others, denying herself. She lives 'from the outside in', that is, the outside determines how she is on the inside.

Being ourselves and different from others carries with it the risk of feeling ourselves to be alone. Fear dominates us. Following social, cultural, religious or political models seems to offer more security and feeds our sense of belonging, making us feel we form part of a group, be it family, a team, a political party or a community. So we are prepared to submit ourselves to those capable of offering us security and relieving our doubts. That attitude makes generative and open sharing difficult; it feeds dependency instead of mutual flourishing.

Sometimes the price to pay for not taking the risk of being oneself is high. Happiness seems further and further away. You don't flourish. To transcend this weakening dynamic, we must dare to concede inner power to ourselves, to nurture ourselves through creativity, and thus overcome paralysing fears. Anna, at 35 years old, had achieved everything she desired. Nevertheless, she was flooded by an unexplainable sadness. In my accompanying of her she discovered that, on her road to becoming so successful, she had renounced her freedom and the development of her full potential. Now, as she risks giving herself the power to unleash her potential, laughter and happiness are returning to her life. You have to take that step, given that if not, the state of loneliness, insecurity and impotence caused by an inner void and emptiness of meaning, when creativity is atrophied and emotions are blocked, can be unbearable. To overcome it, one has two options: conquer this situation or succumb to it.

We succumb to the situation when, out of fear of loneliness, we flee from it. We hide it with the daily routine of activities and seek approval in relationships, in professional success, or in other ways that provide a distraction. As, for example, with Facebook and remaining glued to the Internet for hours. But whistling in the dark does not attract the light. The loneliness, the fear and the anguish remain. Then the person, insecure of themselves, cannot bear the burden that freedom imposes on them and flees from it, looking for escape mechanisms. They abandon their freedom and try to overcome loneliness by generating dependencies.

We keep relationships dependent, and at the same time we seek spaces of freedom. Because of this, many relationships are transitory unions and separations. Love comes to be considered a connection more than a communication or a bond that makes us flourish. Although we are together, we feel divided, and inwardly more alone. It is a loneliness in which one feels a lack of affection and understanding; even though the other is present, they are not there in full awareness. Attitudes of comparison, jealousy, anger and emotional illiteracy separate us. In our living together we realise that our egos collide, suffer and blame. Egos control, dominate and irritate. They desire constantly and are dissatisfied. If we are alone we don't see all the dimensions of our ego and, therefore, we cannot transcend it. Shared living is necessary in order to see oneself in the mirror, learn and let go of the layers that cover over our true potential.

## Shared Living (*Convivencia*)*

Being present, participating and collaborating with others inspires and challenges us in a way that cannot happen to us if we are alone and unconnected to others. However, when someone else exercises power over us, we might react by losing control over our emotions. If we want to flourish we need to learn to free ourselves of guilt, complaints and excuses, and know how to manage anger.

To break the cycle whereby through fear of loneliness we make bonds of dependence (and from that dependence our egos control and bring about anger and pain), let us be aware of the need to cooperate, live in solidarity and have values that open us up to the other and to the world. It is about having a wide and global vision, and breaking out of a closed and self-centred perspective. It means changing our patterns of behaviour and acting out of generosity, no longer being needy, clingy and dependent people. Let us cultivate our inner space and go out into the world to spread wisdom, compassion, solidarity, love, tolerance, acceptance, understanding and unity.

We cannot give to others when we feel weakened by the heaviness of the world and by the atmosphere of a weary world. We can only give to others when we have got our mental, emotional and spiritual power back. On leaning into the power of our presence, we can live together more easily, in a continuous learning that strengthens us and enriches us. We should become aware of our capacity to share and be together in a more whole way.

Strengthened mentally, emotionally and spiritually, we go forward towards a state of flourishing that opens the way towards wholeness, taking loving command of ourselves and making spontaneous connections with the world in love and in work, in the genuine expression of our emotional, sensitive and intellectual faculties. In this way we join with others, with nature and with ourselves, without giving up the integrity of our being. We can live together and share, also living a full solitude that gives us time and space for creativity, art, reflection and meditation. That way we will thrive both when alone and with others.

True inner power is developed by those who live and work in relation to other people, not those who distance themselves from others. We do things for others that we would not do for ourselves. On relating to each other, we widen our mental limits and make our hearts bigger. In relationships and in shared living, our ego defences and the games played by the personality are activated, leading to us to greater awareness and consciousness, and, therefore, to greater personal growth and development. In shared living, we bring our inner qualities and powers into play: tolerance, the capacity to adapt, listen, understand, shape ourselves, forgive, communicate, flow, discern, not be influenced and not depend. When we develop the appreciative stance our living together is kinder. We learn to be and to love in a broader way.

* Translator's note: The term "convivencia" has crossed from the Spanish language into other cultures to refer to a concept of shared living that places emphasis on the relational nature of human beings and their mutual need for one another and for ways to live harmoniously together. It does not necessarily indicate a physical living together, therefore. It is not yet widely used in English and so in this text we use the term "shared living" in an attempt to transmit something of the original "convivencia".

# 10. Sharing in wholeness[10]

What would it be like if our relationships were to flourish? How would new and revitalizing energy flow in our exchanges? Relationships are renewed when each person in the relationship is linked to their essence and connected to their being. They have done their inner work and have a rich personal dialogue, generally manifesting themselves as a person of integrity. They don't need the other out of selfish motives, nor do they need to hide in them; instead, they complement each other. Thus, an option of peaceful and enriching shared living is created in the present and for the future.

Meeting the other out of the wholeness of our being offers us a creative and complementary bond. As long as we are meeting the other out of our dependent needs or our deficiencies, relationships will continue to be nests of conflicts and misunderstandings.

When as men and women we live in our essential being, we will work together as partners in the creation of a new world. We will let the old ego-driven structures fall definitively, making room for a new creation. In doing this we will find the inner power to change the mandates that constitute gender identity in our culture. Until they are transformed, in the working world too, there will not be room for compassion, sisterhood, fraternity, transcendence, spirituality, humanism and a space for otherness.

We will change the paradigm of work as a means of production through generating spaces of creativity, where deep bonding, solidarity, and an opening to transcendence also have their place. A transcendence that does not lessen productivity, but rather improves it with quality, integrity and equanimity, giving meaning and abundance to our lives and our relationships.

Let's realise for once and for all that sharing power does not mean losing it. This is the cooperation that is necessary. Let us create spaces of human enrichment, settings open to the service of the other and the planet with all its inhabitants. Let us become points of reference for a new leadership: appreciative, inspiring, transforming, generous, welcoming, creative and brilliant.

The people who have woken up to this essential new way of being, without masks, with humility and personal power, without submission, with these new thoughts, feelings, attitudes and values, will come together in a harmonious manner. Naturally, they will join to create a new culture that will flourish, one that is appreciative, generous and whole. There will be complementarity between people, not competition or jealousy. Neither victims nor aggressors; neither oppressed nor oppressors. We will be partners.

As women and men who are established in this way of living together, let us see this new world, one in which we flourish in shared living. To do so, we might ask:

- What would it be like if our relationships were to be spaces of mutual flourishing?
- What would relationships be like? What would be different in our way of relating to each other? What new practices would we introduce?
- How would we deliver education?
- How would we share talent and creativity?
- How would we govern?
- What would communications be like?
- What would the workplaces and environment in which we would feel we could flourish be like?
- How to live together in a flourishing way?
- How to create relationships, places and environments that facilitate human flourishing?

Let's explore these questions and the possibilities that they open up. Let's visualise. Let's tap into our inner power, generate a vision, believe in it and share it in order to make it reality, out of respect and cooperation. If we don't believe in it, we won't see it or be able to embody it in reality.

What would it be like if we shared our dreams more and lived out our shared dreams? If we share them, we will have one same purpose: a better world for everyone, a world in which relationships flourish in their surroundings and contribute to a flourishing environment.

This will come about because each person will have done their real and transforming inquiry, in the laboratory of their life. With practice and experience, we will be on the same vibratory wave. We will live non-violence as a lifestyle based on respect for all living beings. We will share values. We will live our full awareness collectively.

We will understand each other without having to explain things a hundred times.

We will experience a practical telepathy, being able to communicate our thoughts and understand each other. Our internal antennae, our consciences and minds, will be clean of unnecessary thoughts and upsetting noises. Listening will be complete. That is, we will listen from the heart, not only from the head and reason.

We will be a group of people working together with a collective conscience to create a new world. In this way we will manage to cooperate out of a shared living that will be an 'us', and not a sum of 'me's. Creating this new world depends on me, on you and on everyone. Get going. When you change, the world will change.

## Understanding

> When we know who we are and what we want, relationships with others will be simpler and more natural for us.[11]
> – Wendy Bristol

> Those that wish to create a new culture, a new society, a new state of things, should first understand themselves. The important thing is for each one to understand themselves in their relationship with another.[12]
>
> – Jiddu Krishnamurti

Let us explore how to increase and broaden our level of understanding. Understanding is necessary in order to relate to the other without losing yourself in them. Sometimes the other influences you in such a way that you lose your core, your centre. If you understand yourself better, you will find it easier to stay faithful to yourself and your principles. That way, in relationship with the other, you don't betray your principles. You remain faithful to yourself. What does this fidelity to yourself mean? Faithful to which part of yourself? You can be faithful to what you would like to be, or faithful to your constant desire for being, faithful to what you have been, faithful to a memory of yourself that you keep as memento, a picture inside you. You can be faithful to an agreement or a way of acting. It is possible to be faithful to what you want to be and not to what you have been. It is a question of being aware of what happens in you on being in the presence of the other; remaining in your centre yet open at the same time to understand and receive.

When you understand yourself, it is easier to understand the other. Understanding helps you to stay faithful and committed to an agreement with yourself and with the other. Only when you understand your relationship with the other will you be able to understand your relationship with the whole, with society. The consequences of relating out of misunderstanding are mistrust, fighting, antagonism, confusion, infidelity, dividedness and duality. Developing understanding requires attention, full awareness, active listening, looking at and seeing oneself, in order to awaken together with the other so that the relationship is a process of self-revelation.

Relating to the other out of personal understanding is the path to liberation, as Krishnamurti explains:[13]

> When one understands oneself in relation to another, the relationship does not turn into a process of isolation, but rather into a movement that allows us to discover our own motives, our own thoughts, our own searches; and that discovery is the beginning of liberation and transformation. Only this immediate transformation can give origin to the fundamental, radical, revolution that is so indispensable in the world. Revolution inside separated walls is not revolution. Revolution only comes when the separation walls are destroyed. That is possible only when one is no longer seeking power.

We can ally ourselves and form a team, sharing the power like Jazz bands do, whose musicians alternate between being the solo and being the followers of the solo. That way we will support each other in playing the game of life together. Shared power generates co-responsibility, complicity and co-creation. Good relationships are those in which we add up and, together, we are better. We stop comparing, competing, criticising and being jealous. We move on to cooperate, join together, value and support one another. We are partners in creating a better reality for everybody.

One of the aspects that prevents us from creating and living out this complicity is the primordial instinct to protect our individual self and be ourselves. That is why we try not to let ourselves feel invaded, attacked, bothered or dominated by others. This leads us to want to defend our terrain and move within a defined individual space. That is why sometimes we reject others and, with our attitudes, we give out messages such as: "Don't come close, don't bother me." The end repercussion of this is that we are alone and isolated.

On living together with others we haven't learned that one of the spaces important to know, connect to and define is the inner space. When we cultivate the inner space of the self, we become aware that nobody can take away from us what we are, or our inner qualities; we can feel comfortable amongst the multitude and not have to defend our space because our assertive attitude and the connection with our positive core protects us. We feel love for ourselves and for the other.

"True self-esteem," explains Branden,[14] "is how we feel with ourselves when not everything goes right. This means when the unexpected challenges us, when others disagree with us, when we have no resources, when the shelter of the group can no longer protect us from the tasks and risks of life, when we have to think, choose, decide and act and nobody guides us or applauds us. In those moments our deepest premises are revealed.

One of the biggest lies we have been told is that it is 'easy' to be selfish and that sacrifice means spiritual strength. When in fact people sacrifice themselves thousands of times a day, including their own conscience. This is their tragedy. Respecting oneself – respecting one's own mind, criteria, values and convictions – is the ultimate act of courage. We see how rare it is. But it is what self-esteem demands of us."

## Cultivating good feelings

Let us learn the art of loving, of being free and allowing others to be. Authentic love flows freely, it is healing and never wounds. You give yourself to the other. It is a self-giving where you share of yourself without denying yourself or sacrificing your positive core (chapter 2). You transcend your 'I-ego' without in so doing losing yourself or getting stuck on to the other. To reach that state in a relationship one needs maturity and personal evolution. The majority of people love each other and tie each other down. When we lose freedom, happiness becomes a distant memory and well-being gives way to unhappiness and to 'bad times'.

Self-knowledge makes it easier to move on from fear to a way of loving that is richer, more tolerant and relaxed. Emotional love can flourish into true lasting love as the initial fire of the emotions grows cooler and is substituted by a wiser and more mature perception. True love needs a fresh and renewing atmosphere, one without fears.

To free ourselves of the tendency to depend, we should have a strong heart, one capable of renouncing selfishness; a heart with nothing to hide, thus leaving the mind free and fearless; a heart that is always prepared to accept new data and change, not clinging on to closed beliefs or obsolete data. With appreciative inquiry we learn to discover the potential and strengths that lie within us and are embedded in our relational system. We discover what there is in the past that empowers us to live our dreams. We learn to design provocative proposals that open our eyes and heart, strengthening our mind to believe that it is possible and enabling our will to achieve it.

With a preoccupied mind and a closed heart, we cannot see and receive new ideas, opportunities and even people into our life. Let us learn to let go of the past and forgive in order to live wholeness in shared living in this moment. It is about cultivating good feelings and cleansing ourselves of bitterness. In cultivating values such as peace, serenity, love, freedom and solidarity, we will overcome deficiencies and feel stronger. Such a heart ends up becoming a lamp that dissipates the dark. A heart like that lives in the now. The return to the now means to embrace what you are and what the other is, and welcome the present moment. You usually mould your expectations according to situations and to people. However, you can shape your life to be open to receiving it. When you receive, you give, you give 'yourself', and in this giving you receive once again. In this reciprocity a dance of joy is created. We flourish together.

# 11. Coaching to flourish

In a process of individual coaching, the coach and the client together can achieve much: the clarification of ideas; new perspectives as to what should and should not be done; a reconnection to strengths and abilities. In most sessions we are successful in this, and the client has understood the impact of some of the behaviours that they need to improve or want to change, creating plans to achieve it and feeling sure of themselves and their ability to do it.

The surprise comes when we receive contrary reactions from the people surrounding the client, their colleagues, bosses and subordinates or their customers, or, even, their family and friends. People who apparently wanted that person to change now show their resistance and scepticism. They pour doubt on to their behaviour, saying: "This isn't him, you can tell he is acting," "This won't last."

The coaching sessions went well, better than well; learning took place, and a commitment to moving forward was forged. However, what was not included on the map, the vision, was the impact of the client's relationships and environment. This situation could have been avoided by applying appreciative inquiry coaching and the principle of social constructionism. This would have meant involving key people in the client's relational network in generative conversations. Conversations in which to talk about: What dreams do we share with those who are in this project with us? The implicated person, which in the case of coaching would be the client, or the person who is accompanied, might ask them: When did you feel at your best with me, what experiences have you had? What was happening? In what way did I facilitate those experiences? What characteristics of my person contributed to you feeling better? How can you help me to strengthen those aspects of my personality so that we might have better experiences? If my behaviour was at its best, how would it be? What would be happening?

If, in the coaching sessions, we only take into account the experiences, ideas and wishes of the client, we won't be helping them to create a support network that helps them in their new steps. It is difficult to change when faced with what needs to be let go of, and the fears brought about by the uncertainty of what will happen; if we add to this the resistance of the people that surround the client, change becomes an even bigger challenge.

The same applies to relationships of friendship or family. When you talk to a friend, you take their relational and family networks into account. They are not an individual isolated from their environment. Therefore, we include the perspectives of the relational matrix of our friend in our conversations.

Concerning these relational perspectives, Kenneth J. Gergen offers this example:

> Similarly, if one is suffering from depression, we focus on the individual mind as the site of repair. If one's job is boring and her boss a tyrant, why should she be treated for her feelings of depression? Why not change the working conditions? In broader terms the individualist presumption operates like a blinder. It is a crude and simplistic way of reacting to problem behavior. We fail to explore the broader circumstances in which actions are enmeshed, and focus all too intensely on the psychological condition of the single individual. Not only is this approach highly limited, but if the broader circumstances of our lives are not addressed it could also be disastrous.[15]

When the people that surround, work or live with the person, in this case, the client, are not up to date with their intentions, and do not live their process of change nor understand their plans for the present and future, they will question and resist, or they might even be in opposition. They weren't given preparation to understand or support the changes that they themselves might have wanted too; they weren't included in the process, they are lacking information and feel disconnected from it. They have felt excluded and don't understand how the changes have come about or what they are for.

In the coaching sessions we can help the person to see what conversations they need to have and who with. Who are the people necessary to making it easier to realise their objectives? Who are the ones making it difficult? What do they need to talk about, and who with, to bring about a change of direction that allows the client to flourish in and with their environment.

## Social constructionism

Social constructionism makes us aware of the importance of our relational network. We construct reality together. Changing just one piece in the relational puzzle brings about many changes. If we include other key pieces of the puzzle in the vision of our coaching sessions, such as the relationships of the client's primary network, the change will be more manageable, more sustainable and successful. It is a matter of living to your full potential together with the other, not in an isolated way. Then, the client will feel understood and supported, and will understand and support in return.

Kenneth J. Gergen and Mary Gergen (2004)[16] describe social constructionism as:

> the creation of meaning through our collaborative activities; and while we converse, we listen to new voices, we ask questions and we reflect on alternative metaphors… we cross a threshold that leads us to new worlds of meaning and sense. Our future is there for us to create it together.

Social constructionism makes us aware of the fact that there are multiple perspectives, and that to bear them in mind enriches us and allows the collective wisdom to flourish and be shared. Social constructionism is based on the fact that:

- We create our ways of understanding reality and values according to the language we use.
- There are multiple traditions with which to construct the world.
- We exist within multiple realities and together can co-construct new realities.
- Words create worlds.
- We accept impermanence.
- Social realities are not fixed.
- All knowledge is saturated with values, conventionalisms, theories, time and space.
- The ways of explaining emerge from relationships.
- All social action is open to multiple meanings.
- Alterations in our linguistic practices are powerful.

Appreciative inquiry proposes constructing the new in organisational development and our relational systems, where:

- Innovation eclipses intervention.
- Creating substitutes resolving.
- The emphasis is on collaborative leadership.
- We accentuate positive assumptions about human beings.
- Attention is placed on dialogue more than diagnosis.

On innovating, creating, collaborating, assuming the positive and dialoguing, we create a fertile generative field.

The individual contribution to a team offers a creative impulse that flourishes with the support of the community. When the members of a community or team create together, anything is possible. We are all affected one way or another by the social or organisational system we belong to, and, in the same way, our individual actions influence others and depend on them to a certain extent. When we are aware of this interaction and recognise its value, not only will we think about what we want on an individual level, but we will take others into account. We will consider how achieving our objectives will influence them, and, vice versa, how they can influence us, and how that influence can strengthen us all positively and benefit the world.

When the coach recognises that each person forms an integral part of a whole, that is, of multiple relationships, they can accompany the client in a real and significant change. It is a question of dialoguing, of using the narrative principle (of narrating significant stories with a language that emphasises what has been and is life-giving for us), and of living a process openly. We should include in the process those people that offer the client perspective, relevance, and even critique, and whose support is important for them to create meaning and achieve the goals they have set for themselves. It is a matter of taking into account that: "Through relational processes we create the world we want to live and work in," states Kenneth Gergen.[17] "The dialogue of social constructionism deals with the processes in which as human beings we generate sense and meaning together. Our focus is on how social groups and relational practices in groups create and sustain beliefs in reality, in the rational and in the good. We recognise that in the measure that people create meaning, we are sowing seeds for action. The meaning of the action is interlaced. As we generate meaning together, we create the future."

## Generative conversations

At the core of appreciative inquiry is the promotion of conversations that provide sense, generate meaning and move the energy necessary to create the desired future. They are generative conversations. What do they generate? Many positive experiences! For example: empathy, trust, dreams, commitment, letting go of wounds, flowing, sense and meaning; and, in essence: fulfilment. On an organisational level, they generate: commitment, excitement, new products, new ways of relating to each other, better communication, better results for people, products and the planet.

A conversation is generative when we help each other to see 'what could be' and 'what is possible'. This shared vision attracts us and motivates us to undertake actions together. They are actions that have meaning and bring significance to our lives, our relationships and our organisations. They are actions for a common good motivated by a shared vision.

As a coach, I accompany the person in opening up generative conversations that allow them to express their full potential in their social relational context. I suggest to them the need to involve others, the people who are appropriate to work with him or her in supporting them in their desired achievements. We see what conversations are necessary, with whom and when. We create an appreciative tone that allows for the encouragement of the best in each person, and in what they can create together.

The appreciative tone is created by setting out a framework in which we can foster the valuing of people in the organisation, in the community or in the family system. I ask questions that allow the client to value how the people in their environment have contributed in the best moments. It is about the person developing an appreciative way of looking at his or her surroundings.

I also establish the need to have conversations that develop the appreciative view of the members of the organisation or their family towards the client. We achieve this by asking questions that awaken that view. We explain to the people significant for the client that we are going to invest in some coaching sessions for this person, asking them when they were in their best form – what were they doing and what occurred as a result of their actions? We are going to invest in maximizing their potential;

let's imagine that the person gives the best of themselves – what would the manifestation of the best of themselves be like? What will they be doing and how will they do it? On including the vision of others, we broaden perspectives.

I can ask a manager or colleague of my client to tell me the story of when the most effective moment was when they gave him or her feedback. In this way, the manager or colleague becomes aware of what and how the best way of giving them feedback is, and what happens when they give it that way. I can also ask them to tell me a story of when they supported my client's ability to be successful. Or I can ask the client's team – what are the challenges that you now need to deal with, and in what way can you be thinking partners yourselves in order to overcome them? Although this question seems to focus at first on the challenges, the intention is to set up a generative conversation about how to support each other by being thinking partners (chapter 21).

In this sense, appreciative coaching offers a radical difference in the context of traditional coaching. Radical, because in the majority of traditional coaching agreements, the confidentiality of the whole process is maintained between the coach and the client. When we propose involving others in the process, we are opening it to an exchange that stops being private, permitting a flow of conversations, meanings and actions between the client and their network of necessary relationships.

It is about constructing healthy relationships by involving people in the setting of what is worked with in the coaching. What people should we involve? It depends on whether we are in a process of coaching that is for work, professional, or of a team or life. In the latter, it will be important to involve some member of the family, a good friend, a work partner or colleague with whom the person works or shares their properties and projects. If it is a process of coaching by objectives, in which the client wants to develop certain projects in an organisation, we could include the boss of the client or their colleagues, co-workers, members of their team, customers and mentors.

This does not mean that all these people come with the client. In the coaching sessions, we ask questions that allow the client to have the necessary conversations with those people that will influence and be decisive in their well-being and that of all the system. I help the person to prepare appreciative interviews, in such a way that the appreciative tone is assured, making the conversation more manageable, above all in the cases where the relationship is not optimal. When the client feels very uncomfortable with a person they have to interview or should converse with, the coach can intervene in order to prepare the ground.

Throughout the different phases of the appreciative coaching, we ask questions that the person can transfer to their relational network in order to incorporate the vision and perspective of others. With this we achieve a broadening of their vision, which includes others and makes them see the importance of their support for the sustainability of the process of change that they are going through. In the process they learn to create and ask appreciative questions that stimulate transforming conversations. The change takes on other tones and directions, thanks to the breadth of perspectives incorporated.

For example, let's consider the case that Kenneth Gergen tells us about, whereby:

> a client speaks at length of her anger at her husband's irresponsibility. How might a therapist respond? She might, for one, pause, and ask, "Can you tell me some ways your husband is actually responsible?" As a second possibility, she might say, "How often do you have these feelings of anger?" As a third possibility, she might inquire, "You know, I wonder if it's not really anger you are feeling, but an insecurity; it just gets expressed as anger."
>
> What is it that the woman has expressed? In the first

> option, the therapist or coach has paid attention to the husband's behavior; anger recedes into the background. The second has brought the client's anger into focus, and the husband's behavior recedes in importance. Yet, in the third option, the coach or therapist has treated her words of anger as expressions of insecurity. So, what then has the woman expressed? It depends on the therapist's reply and on the question that is asked. The woman, in this case the client, furnishes the possibility for meaning, but the shape of this meaning is furnished by the therapist. At the same time, the therapist's words only make sense in light of what the client has spoken. None of these responses would make sense if the client had simply been staring at the ceiling. In effect, neither client nor the coach nor therapist makes sense without the other, and the particular sense that results requires the coordination of their efforts. Therefore, what takes place in the conversation is constructed between those that participate in it, it is a process of co-action, that is, of co-ordinated action.[18]

As a coach, I improve my capacity when I recognise the different perspectives and the multiplicity of possible interpretations of the stories that the person expresses. Of all of them, I choose the most relevant and generative aspects that support their choice and growth. And when they talk to me about a situation I ask them what perspective they want to deal with it from. Following the previous example, it would be to ask them, in option 1, do you want us to focus on creating images of possibilities that your husband is – might be – responsible? In the second option the question would be – do you want us to focus on what you feel, on your anger? And in looking at the occasions on which you overcame your anger, what strengths did you use to do so? Or, third, putting your anger in the background and inquiring more deeply into what you feel, and in discovering moments of security and wholeness in your life, when the insecurity and anger dissolved or were overcome.

The person who lives through the conversations with me, and when it applies, the coaching process, learns to ask appreciative and generative questions that continue to help them after having finished the coaching process. It is about helping them to develop lenses of social constructionism with questions such as: What stories do I tell myself and which do I tell others? What do I say to myself and to others? How could these stories be more generative? What can I ask others in order to involve them? What can I ask them so that they contribute in the fulfilment of our desired future? What missing question needs to be asked that will open us up to a new dialogue once we ask it? What other point of view can I apply to this situation? How would it change if I did so?

In organisations, systems, communities and families, we refer to the socially constructed environment and to the belief system and perceptions, like organisational culture. In the appreciative coaching of teams and organisations we propose a change of culture and an improvement of climate by applying the principles (chapter 14) through the five phases explored in chapter 16.

# Part III

# Appreciative Inquiry Coaching

When strength touches strength, or hope touches hope, or the inspiration of one touches the inspiration of another – and when this ratio reaches near the 4:1 level – then instead of languishing, human systems tap into the upward spiral of mutual elevation or mutual upbuilding. There is a positive contagion or spread, like a spark of inspiration turning into a flame, and that flame becoming an Olympian torch or legacy.
– David Cooperrider[19]

# 12. Appreciative inquiry coaching

So far, we have seen the multiple possible perspectives in accompanying someone, be it a friend, family member, colleague, or client, in moving forwards towards connecting to their essence and expressing their full potential. We have dealt with the importance of opening the door, the paths within, and broadening our ways of looking; the value of appreciation and of flourishing together in our environment. Everything covered in parts I and II of this book serves as a basis for understanding and practising appreciative inquiry coaching, and improving the way we accompany people.

Appreciative inquiry coaching has its foundations in appreciative inquiry. To increase your knowledge of the history of appreciative inquiry, what it covers and how to apply it in organisations, you can complement this book with the one I published jointly with David Cooperrider, the creator of appreciative inquiry, *Indagación apreciativa: un enfoque innovador para la transformación personal y de las organizaciones* (2013). Let's look now in brief at what it consists of.

## Appreciative inquiry

Appreciative inquiry is a process and methodology that fosters change. It increases strengths, converting them into habits, and promotes growth, excitement and motivation. Appreciative inquiry proposes intervening in organisations from an innovative approach, bringing together vision, imagination, knowledge, commitment and speed in transformation, strategic change and sustainable growth in organisations and communities. It is applied at all levels and in all spheres: personal, team, social, political, business, organisational, educational, sanitary, religious and cultural, amongst others. The breadth of possibilities that it offers helps us to discover that we have a great potential to generate a better reality for everyone.

Appreciative inquiry is a process of shared search that is centred on the positive core (see pages 11) of an organisation, group, system or person. It seeks to connect people and the organisation to their competences, skills, talents, and to their best achievements and practices. "In their broadest focus," states David Cooperrider, "it implies a systematic discovery of what gives life to a living system when it is in its most vital, most effective and capable moment for constructing in economic, ecological and human terms."[20]

With appreciative inquiry, we see organisations and relationships as spaces of possibilities, where we find strengths, aspects to be conserved, and others needing to be questioned or changed. The change arises out of aspirations and focusing on what we most want, instead of what we don't want.

To sum up, we can say that appreciative inquiry contributes to fostering change; to increasing strengths and turning them into habits; to promoting growth, excitement and motivation; to creating an exceptional climate and to innovating for strategic change and sustainable growth. It connects people and organisations to their competences, skills, talents and their best achievements and practices, enabling them to translate images of possibilities into reality and beliefs into practices.

## Appreciative Inquiry coaching[21]

Appreciative Inquiry (AI) coaching energises positive change in a person or team. As a process, it facilitates discovering, expanding and sustaining the roots of their success, creating an attractive image of their desired future and designing concrete plans in order to carry out their wishes and dreams. On defining change as positive I am referring to the fact that in general all change brings pain, sorrow and anxiety, which is why, in AI coaching, we focus on what a person longs for, the images of the future that attract them and what they most want. With this approach we succeed in raising levels of enthusiasm and positive energy, and reducing the anxiety caused by change. In AI coaching we put the spotlight on the values and deepest longings of the person and the team. People are connected and reconnected to their essence, their positive core and their strengths and abilities.

On accompanying a person, we involve in our range of vision and conversations other people whose support is important in achieving what the client wants. This will have been previously defined. Special care is taken to align the networks of social support of the person undertaking the process of appreciative coaching – who we call the client, as I explained in the introduction – in contributing to the learning of the members of their relational circle, sharing their dreams and support for positive change. This is achieved by constructing strong and resilient relationships with the people of their main network or those that are relevant for the client. The primary network is made up of the closest people, family, friends and colleagues.

One aspect to bear in mind in the sessions is that the client's declarations and statements do not originate in their independent mind, but are rather the fruit of their relational process. "This process, then," says Gergen, "invites caring attention. By the same token, the therapist or counselor is not responsible solely to the client, but to the entire web of relations carried by the client into the consultation chamber. It is not enough to assist the client in moving into a new pattern of action; one must also attend to the ramifications of this pattern within the relational matrix to which the client returns."[22]

We are introducing a relational point of view. It is not only the person that we see, but also all their relational fabric, and how they influence and enrich one another mutually. Social constructionism makes us aware that there is not one single truth, but rather multiple points of view. When the client talks to us, we can ask them questions encouraging them to see beyond their perspective, and thus to take their relational matrix into account.

This consideration of the relational network is one of the foundations of appreciative inquiry based on social constructionism (page 64). As well, in the sessions and encounters we apply appreciative principles, the phases of appreciative inquiry, appreciative questions and generative conversations. We take into account a change in the use of language, that is, of leaving behind the language of lack and bringing in a language of abundance, as I explained in chapter 8. We include the motivating power of images in the fulfilment of what the client wants. I will be explaining more about this in the following chapters.

In the sessions of appreciative inquiry coaching we look for and focus on what we most want, not what we don't want (for example, if someone wants to stop eating sweets and cake they concentrate on what they want: more health, more exercise, greater flexibility, etc., and with the vision of the objective that attracts them, they find the power to leave behind what they don't want). That way we develop the capacity to visualise the best of what we are and of what we want. This fosters the positive inner dialogue that increases mental capacity and positive emotionality, facilitating, what is more, better leadership and teamwork.

Richard Boyatzis, the creator of coaching by compassion, works at the same university as David Cooperrider, one of the originators of Appreciative Inquiry. Boyatzis, together with other researchers, has studied the psychophysiological effect that appreciative inquiry coaching and coaching with compassion produce, unlike coaching for accomplishment. In AI coaching and coaching with compassion, the relationship between the coach and the client is important, generating an appreciative bond that fosters positive emotions and awakens the person's dreams and longings. In conversations, we forge a bond between the client's longings and the images that attract them towards the future they aspire to. Once the person has clear images and is connected to them, we design proposals of principles and actions that will lead them towards living out their longings. In coaching by accomplishment, however, objectives are set and plans are laid out to be fulfilled. It is much more aimed at action and does not necessarily take into account images of the future, the relational network, or the strengthening of positive emotions.

"When we focus on the vision for the future that the client has, we evoke the experiences that encourage the positive emotional attractor that their dreams, values and passions generate. That way the parasympathetic nervous system is stimulated, which has the job of stimulating various endocrine glands that are associated to many benefits for the human being."[23] Appreciative inquiry coaching is based on processes focused on people's positive core and searching for and discovering the images of past and future experience that nurture it and make it flourish. With these processes we stimulate vitality, hope and personal and relational power.

In the first encounters between coach and client, we define the subject or topics that they want to deal with in the sessions. They are defined in affirmative and positive terms, following the guidelines of the phase of Defining of appreciative inquiry in coaching. Following that, they go on to the phase of Discovering and, then, to the Dream phase, in which the coach helps the client to find their positive images of the future. The aspirations of the client are reflected in these images, which we call guiding images, given that they will sustain the enthusiasm and motivation necessary to uphold the actions that will lead them towards achieving their wishes. The affirmative images of the future, whereby the client affirms themselves in order to move forward towards fulfilling them, are key to the evolution and sustainability of the process. In this aspect, AI coaching and coaching with compassion meet one another.

In coaching with compassion, as in AI coaching, the other is accompanied in achieving their dreams and fulfilling their aims and passions. One focuses on invocating those aspects of the person, which Boyatzis calls "Ideal self", to begin and guide the process of change. The ideal self is the individual vision of what the person wants to be and it reflects their deepest aspirations. The focus is on helping the client to articulate their vision or their dreams. It has been shown, by the research into positive vision, how this leads to the creation of new neural pathways that help to guide future behaviour (Roffe, Schmidt and Ernst, 2005)[24] and foster hope. That is, that we are changing mental habits thanks to invoking positive images that attract the future, which we call guiding images.

An appreciative inquiry coach helps people to define what it is that they want to see grow in their lives. It is possible that their ideal self is the self in its essence, its positive core. And possibly, this forms part of what they want to see grow and flourish. The coach motivates them to discover and recognise their talents and skills in order to construct, from them, the declarations of possibilities and actions that will lead them towards achieving their desires. In this way, they can accompany them in designing proposals of possibilities that contribute to embodying their guiding images in their reality.

This approach increases positive emotions, encouraging the person to take on greater commitments. From the experience of positivity, one can travel the path in a nicer way, in spite of the discomfort and fears that accompany a process of personal and group transformation.

Appreciative Inquiry coaching is based on premises that are also useful for applying to our life and relationships. We shall explore them now.

# 13. Premises

Appreciative Inquiry coaching is based on premises that can be applied to our personal, relational, professional and family lives. I have grouped each set of premises under a theme or area.

## Giving Life

> The essence of appreciative inquiry coaching holds that human systems are heliotropic, meaning they will move toward the generative and creative images that reside in their most positive core – their values, visions, achievements and best practices.
> – Watkins and Mohr (2001)

A heliotropic system is what we see functioning, for example, in the jungle. The plants and trees go up towards the sun and their roots reach out to where there is abundant water. That is, they position themselves and grow towards what gives them life. The appreciative inquiry coach looks for what gives life to people in order to, once found, advance towards it, connecting themselves from the root to their water and sun, rooted in the earth, rising up towards the sky, and considering their relational system; it would be similar to taking into account the plants with which they share spaces and relationship.

## Reality and action

"In every society, organisation, group or individual there is something that works," say Orem, SL; Binkert, J. and Clancy, AL.[25] "What people focus on becomes their reality. Reality is created in the moment and there are multiple realities."

One of the pragmatic and hopeful theories of appreciative inquiry is based on Kurt Lewin's premise that human actions depend on the world we construct, and not on the world as it is. In this sense, we construct our world on the basis of the perspectives created as we go along in response to our relationships and conversations. Bearing the multiplicity of perspectives in mind helps us to keep things relative, to open ourselves to the other, to consider them and to take decisions with a broad mind.

## Relationship

Relationships are at the centre of change and the reality we create. We are the fruit of the relationships that we have had since we were born. Our self is relational. We learn together as we go along. Each person is a relational web; we cannot treat them only considering them as an individual separate from their network. In teamwork and in shared life, we take different voices and points of view into account so as to extend our knowledge and move forward together in mutual recognition.

It is important to value our differences.

## Language

The language that people use creates their reality.

> The limits of my language are the limits of my world.
> – Ludwig Wittgenstein

See chapter 8 on the language of abundance.

## Image

Images create worlds. We create our reality with the images that we believe in and project. Change begins in the images we have of the future.

## Questions

Communities and people move in the direction that their

questions, their issues and their energy lead them in. The act of asking questions influences the group and the person in such a way that they either get stuck or go forward.

Questions mobilise our worlds.

## Appreciate

Appreciating and acknowledging the best of 'what is' awakens our positivity.

Every human being needs to be appreciated and recognised. When we appreciate, we move on; our mind opens up to receive, to recognise new data and to learn. Appreciating, we feel wonder and curiosity. When we appreciate, we discover the best of 'what is' and we open ourselves to seeing 'what could be'. See more on appreciating in chapter 6.

## Positive emotion

Positivity and positive emotions widen people's repertoires of thought and action and build true resources. Barbara Fredrickson (2009)[26] explains: "positivity cannot prevent all bad things from happening to you, just some of them." She defines six vital facts about positivity in our attitudes and emotions which, summing up, say that:

> positivity feels good, positivity doesn't just change the contents of your mind, trading bad thoughts for good ones; it also changes the scope or boundaries of your mind. Positivity transforms your future. Although good feelings will forever be fleeting, over time, positivity literally brings out the best in you. Positivity puts the brakes on negativity, and it works like a re-set button. It obeys a tipping point, that is, its effects are non-linear. A tipping point is that sweet spot in between where a small change makes a big difference. And finally the sixth aspect is that you can increase your positivity. The treasure of your own positivity is waiting.

## Change

People feel more confident and more comfortable on their journey to the future (the unknown) when they take with them parts of the past (the known). If people take parts of their past with them towards the future, these should be the best of their past, in order to create the best future possible.

# 14. Principles

The principles of appreciative inquiry are the philosophical foundation of the strategies for change based on strengths. The phases of appreciative inquiry, the cycle of the five Ds (define, discover, dream, design and destiny) are a way of applying these principles both for personal and organisational development. The five founding principles offer us a practical guide for coaching.

We can apply the principles in coaching sessions without necessarily following the phases. For example, if a person comes to me who is worried about the results they are getting, by applying the principles, I work with their energy and emotions, creating positive emotion. If they have little positive energy, through the principles I will encourage the conversation, filling it with new possibilities. When I see that the conversation that I suggest isn't going anywhere, using the principles I can ask different questions that stimulate other reflections. If they are dejected or despairing, the principles guide me in awakening their courage and confidence. If they are distracted, I will help them to bring back their attention to the moment.

Basing myself on the principles, we manage to open up conversations that help to change the way people perceive and relate to the world, opening up new inspiring possibilities. The person I am accompanying feels strengthened to take on new challenges and to face life from a positive and hopeful perspective. They are enabled to set out towards their dreams, and to be more at peace and happy with themselves, with their past, their present and their future.

The five guiding principles defined in a word are:

- constructionist

- simultaneity
- poetic
- anticipatory
- positive and appreciative

There are another five principles that we call the emerging principles, since they came into being with the practice of appreciative inquiry. Let's see what each principle proposes and how it is applied in coaching.

## Constructionist principle

The constructionist principle is based on the social constructionism that we examined on pages 64–66.

We could summarise the premises of this principle as follows:

- Words create worlds.
- Reality is constructed through language.
- The relationship between words and the worlds we construct with them is negotiable.
- A person's behaviour and actions are affected by and exist in a socially constructed reality.

As a coach using the principle of social constructionism:

- I am aware of the client's best contributions to living to their full potential. It is a potential that lies in the relational process that the client participates in.
- I discover the topics that need to be dealt with in the coaching sessions. The topics arise from a social construction, that is, from the person in their relationship with the coach and the multiple realities constructed through their relationships.
- I stimulate conversations that establish the necessary agreements for real change to happen in practice.

- I open up communication between the client and the people with whom they work and live, in order to construct an agreement, and commitment to the goals they set out for themselves, and to the subjects brought up in the coaching.
- The process undergone in the coaching sessions takes into account the importance of constructing relationships that support the client's action.

## Principle of simultaneity

Conversations and interactions become positive in the instant that we ask a positive question, tell a positive story or share a positive reflection. Change begins the moment we ask the question. "Positive questions and reflections change everything. They are themselves the change we seek to make. They don't just begin a process that leads to a positive future; they simultaneously create a positive present by shifting our conversations and interactions in a positive direction. They are not just a prelude to change; they are change."[27]

The principle of simultaneity holds that:

- The inquiry is the intervention.
- All questions are leading questions.
- Each question, conversation and contact with someone in the system has an impact. Recognising this and appreciating it helps us to value it.
- Thoughts and images are formed with the first question.

In appreciative coaching I start the session by asking questions about the best moments and experiences the person has had. The moment they begin to remember those good times, their facial expression changes, and a smile spreads out on their face. Then I ask questions in relation to their search, to their essential desire, and what they want to achieve, in such a way that they share their longings for the present and the future.

It seems easy, but in practice the tendency is to talk about difficulty and what is not going well. We inhabit a cultural environment in which it is habitual to focus on what is missing, what doesn't work, what is done badly. Nevertheless, I don't go down that route. And when, almost straightaway, the person returns to what doesn't work, what they are lacking, what isn't working, I redirect the conversation again with another question so that little by little they start to focus on discovering their positive core and what they want.

"And it is in every moment that we are changing and influencing change. AI coaching is mindful that, moment to moment, in every question we ask or statement we make, we are creating the future for good or ill."[28] That is why I try to create a strong bond between the person and the images of what they want, so as to weaken their bond with what is difficult or makes them ill. That way, the feeling and the belief emerge that I can, and we can.

## Poetic principle

With the daily demands of productivity, action and resolution, and the data we are flooded with through information and noise, it is easy to lose creativity, inspiration, poetry, beauty and the artistic. In appreciative coaching sessions, we look to give a voice to the creative and poetic impulse that has in some way been buried inside the person. We look to illuminate their dreams and aspirations, what they desired and didn't persevere in achieving, due to pressures and other reasons, to the artist that lies inside them and wants to be reborn.

The more we attend to the positive dimensions of the present moment, the more positive our intentions for the next and future moments will be. Being aware of what adds richness, texture, depth, beauty, meaning and energy to our life awakens a magnificent potential in us.

It is not that problems disappear, but on attending to and feeling the poetry of life, with its textures and musicality, we focus on other aspects that are more meaningful and essential. We accumulate the energy and vitality that help us to deal with problems from another perspective with a positive and generative attitude.

The poetic principle holds that what we focus on grows. If we focus on what doesn't work and is problematic, problems increase. If we focus on problems, we create more problems. Focusing on successes will generate more successes.

With the poetic principle, the coach:

- Looks for the best stories of the client and their system.
- Helps the client to see themselves as more whole and complete.
- Remains open to interpretation and to diverse stories.
- Recognises and values multiple realities.
- Incites an evocative language in order to involve heart and head, body and feeling, remembering and evoking, recollecting and imagining.

Poetry, unlike an academic text, invites us to multiple interpretations. And life is like that too: like a poem open to be interpreted in diverse ways, according to your state of mind, the moment and who you are with while you read it. In coaching, we give voice to the multiple interpretations and to different perspectives, so that we expand the way that we understand and live reality, making room for new possibilities. In sum, the poetic principle accompanies us in social constructionism, affirming that there is not one single point of view, but rather multiple perspectives, and we appreciate the different realities that these latter create, staying open to the possible interpretations and meanings that they engender.

The coach helps the client to see themselves from a broader perspective and to appreciate behaviours or tendencies that they previously considered to be weaknesses. Now, seeing them from another point of view they can extend the possibilities of being, of the self, be more effective, more luminous, clearer, more creative, opening themselves to their potential in order to flourish. In conversations we evoke a poetic language that can awaken creativity and nudge it to express itself.

## Anticipatory principle

The anticipatory principle holds that our questions and reflections flow from our attitude and the vision we uphold. If our attitude is of despair and our vision is negative, it will be difficult to look for and celebrate what works, and the positive. However, when we observe what things were like in their best moments, and we connect to the positive core that makes us vibrate, it will be easier for us to look for and find images of the future that inspire us. "It takes more than just a vague confidence that everything will be alright; it takes a specific, positive image of the future in order to impact the dynamics of the present."[29] Margaret Wheatley describes vision as a field (1999), and as such "it is a power, not a place, an influence, not a destination."

The anticipatory principle states that:

- Image inspires action.
- We create what we imagine.
- Human systems move towards images of their future.
- Positive images create positive futures.

Applying the anticipatory principle, the coach accompanies the person in capturing their experiences of wholeness and shining, no matter how rare or few they have been. In using those optimum moments to illuminate images of their inspiring future, they create energy and action with which to design and construct their best future.

In the sessions I invite the person to share the images that attract them of the future, including a relational system, to inspire and achieve a level of support possibly without precedents, one that they hadn't even imagined, and that might inspire them to take extraordinary actions for their desired development. People feel grateful to see someone of their relational system sharing what motivates them; they vibrate and are enthused by it. It is easier and quicker to create the desired future if their relationships share in it and support it.

In the Dream phase, we accompany the client in imagining the best possible future, widening their creative and imaginative capacity. Peter Drucker, the great management guru, stated that: "the best way to predict the future is to create it." And to create it, we should first be capable of imagining it. The anticipatory principle accompanies us in this fascinating process of developing the power of the imagination.

People can face changes with greater confidence when their image of the future is rooted in the best of their past, anchored in their personal strengths and actively supported by their managers, colleagues, partners, friends and family.

## Positive appreciative principle

Most people want to enjoy positive actions and good positive results in life, relationships and at work. When we live positive energy and emotions, we weaken the downward spiral, finding more strength to construct, create, overcome and, in sum, face challenges and move forward. On identifying, appreciating, recognising and amplifying their strengths, people go beyond problem solving and focus on what they want and what they want more of. That way they gather strength to leap forward.

Positive energy and emotions broaden our mental capacity, expand our awareness, increase our skills and strengthen our resilience; they help us leave to one side negativity and what consumes us on the inside, creating a spiral of growth and flourishing. With them we are more courageous in letting go of what we need to let go of, making room for the new that is waiting to be born or is already in the process of being born.

The positive principle holds that the negative energy and emotions associated with identifying, analysing and correcting weaknesses lack enough strength to transform systems and make them move in new directions. Maybe in their best applications they will manage to correct problems, but they will be missing the emotion and force that is achieved with the positive images that attract us and pull us forward.

The positive principle evokes the positive core, which consists of strengths, achievements, unexplored potential, skills, talents and values. Building strengths is more effective than correcting weaknesses.

Living and applying the positive principle is to:

- When positive, be unconditionally positive.
- Look for stories of when the client was in their best state, in their excellence, at their greatest moments.
- Create positive and attractive images of the future.
- Live the heliotropic principle: grow towards the light, towards the positive image that illuminates our way.
- People and their systems move towards what they most focus on and inquire into.
- Positive questions and adopting a positive attitude and position can illuminate the longings that were perhaps lost out of cynicism.

The question lies in being aware of where we focus our attention and the consequences of so doing. We can choose to focus on the deficits, the lacks, what doesn't work, or rather we can choose to focus on the strengths, on abundance, on what works. The positive approach can be an antidote in the face of cynicism and the cynic.

In appreciative coaching we focus on strengths and on the positive, even when someone is living in the midst of challenges, problems or complicated situations, which are, in the first instance, what may have led the person to get involved in a coaching process. Each conversation can either embed already existing perceptions, or it can open up an awareness to strengths and new possibilities. Each interaction in appreciative coaching is guided by the positive appreciative principle. We find what we look for; therefore the appreciative coach looks for what is appreciative and positive.

Thanks to the work of Barbara Fredrickson, we are learning more about the impact of the emotions, thoughts and experiences that bring about positivity. We can be the creators of well-being and stop wallowing in unhappiness. Fredrickson has shown how positive emotions expand our awareness, increase our creative capacity and highlight our abilities.

Positive emotions are more inclusive than negative ones. When we feel anger, we reject the other. When we are sad, we shut ourselves off. Contrarily, when we feel joy, love and happiness, we want to share it and include others. Positive emotions help us to change from the 'me' to the 'we'. And from this we/us, we can construct a relational network of support and help that is more robust and sustainable.

Fredrickson[30] has demonstrated, in her multiple pieces of research, that positive emotions and their impact make people flourish and function in an optimum way. When a community or a group of people experience positive emotions collectively, they appreciate strengths and imagine an invigorating future, the positive change is accelerated and the impulse that leads them forward with commitment is sustained.

Fredrickson holds that positive emotions are antidotes to any trace of the effect of negative emotions. This works not only on the level of individual coaching, but also in the social transformation of the system, when this latter is involved in a process of team coaching with appreciative inquiry.

The positive appreciative principle is also applied to how we see problems. Once an appreciative atmosphere has been established in the relationship and coaching session, I consider it sometimes important to have an appreciative approach to the challenge or problem. I can ask questions which bring out the strengths that have helped the clients in difficult situations in the past, and see how the strengths or abilities that arose then can be relevant for the present situation. We inquire into how we can resort to them, how they can help or accompany in resolving what is being lived through now. The fact of valuing what arose in the past and helped them to get through a difficult situation makes someone have a more appreciative vision of themselves and their ability to overcome things. The confidence is strengthened that yes, one can, because one was already able to in the past. We find in the past the aspects that empower us for the present and the future.

Appreciative coaching doesn't dig into problems, it acknowledges them, appreciates them and works with them if they arise, but it doesn't inquire into their causes. Rather, it inquires into what gave someone strength to get out of similar situations that might serve as guidelines to connecting to those inner strengths and capacities in the present. That is, we always inquire into the positive core (page 11), which is life-giving, reinvigorating people to go forward with greater power and lightness, and less heaviness.

Now let's look at the emerging principles.

## Principle of being aware

This is the principle that declares the importance of being aware of oneself and of others. Aware of multiple realities and perspectives. Aware of what you say to yourself and of the impact of your thoughts and conversations. It is to understand and integrate the principles of appreciative inquiry into your life. It means to reflect upon automatic thinking in order to make it non-automatic.

When thoughts are repetitive, they become machine-like and automatic. You run after them like a shadow that won't let go of its object. You think without realising that you are thinking. Repetitive thinking is like a hammer that keeps hitting the nail unceasingly. It is a robotic thinking. It arises from habits, and mental perceptions and creations. With machine-like thinking you lose elasticity, creativity and strength. If, besides, the thinking is negative, it ends up tormenting you and creating problems that don't exist.

As people and as coaches, it is important to be aware of what we think. That our thinking stop being mechanical. To do so, I suggest that you go into silence and transform your automated 'machine'. Step out of the tunnel of your exhausting repetitive thoughts. You create your thoughts. You can change them. Turn your mind into an inspiring creating force, in harmony with your guiding images, and the creator of poetry and beauty. Enjoy your creation, the thoughts you generate. Think what you want to think.

If you gain this mastery over your thinking, you will listen better and your contribution to conversations will be more meaningful. You will be more aware of what is said and what isn't said.

In the sessions of accompaniment I introduce moments of silence which invite reflection and the realisation of what one is thinking. It is a question of extending the moments we are living through by being fully aware; that is, in full consciousness.

## Narrative principle

Stories transform. We construct stories about our lives. We can change our stories to help us bring into being more of what we want. We can change the interpretation of our stories and narrate them with another language and from another point of view.

The stories we tell ourselves over and over again create and perpetuate the reality of our perceptions. These stories have the power to limit our options, but they can also expand the possibilities that we imagine and create.

When the client tells me stories that are heavy and painful, I invite them to tell them from another perspective, valuing what they learned, and what did work. When someone narrates their story from an appreciative perspective, they integrate the past, creating harmony and feeling at peace with it. You live the present better if you are at peace with your past.

## Principle of acting *as if...*

This consists of acting as if you were already living what you want to live. As if the future were the present and your longings were an achieved experience. Try it. Try a behaviour that is aligned with what you want and build from there. "Be the change you want to see in the world," said Gandhi.

In conversations with the client, one can put forward proposals in line with what they see themselves doing and living what they want to be living. We can ask them: What would you be like if you were to live to your full potential? What would you do differently? If you lived more of what you wish to live, what would you feel? Try to evoke those feelings now and live them. If you act as if you were already where you want to be, or were already like how you want to be, you bring out your potential to be and live how you want. We can set out some first steps to acting as if one is already living his or her ideal. And in the coaching sessions these can be specified and agreed on.

## Principle of free choice

Free choice liberates and provides power. Choice through submission, on the other hand, represses us and reduces our personal power. Pressurised by our cultural and relational system, we don't allow ourselves to do what we want and we act out of obligation.

When people are free to choose, they are more committed to performing an action, because they have chosen it and feel it to be theirs. Free choice stimulates excellence and positive change. In appreciative inquiry coaching, we support what the client most longs for so that they give themselves permission and feel good in so doing. Evidently, the support is offered when one is in tune with the values of the other and what is wished for is ethical and non-violent.

"Generative approaches promote freedoms that are conversational resources, generative skills and capacities to visualise the future that can be integrated into diverse approaches and processes," states Dora Fried Schnitman. Some of these freedoms could be summarised in the appreciative inquiry model as:

- Participating proactively in the generation of possibilities and alternatives.
- Creating and constructing a future out of the present.
- Reconstructing oneself, building the identity one most wants and deconstructing what one doesn't want in relation to one's self-image.
- Recuperating and reconstructing relationships in innovative ways, producing possibilities, identities and new relationships.
- Recognising diversity in the apparently habitual.
- Recognising values and resources as shared drivers.
- Recycling and innovating.
- Collaborating, expressing oneself, recovering implicit resources, listening to what is said and expanding on it,

being listened to, sharing and constructing together.
- Building associative and collaborative relationships.

"One of the freedoms that the appreciative approach fosters is that of allowing oneself to be positive. Appreciative inquiry opens up the path for people to feel free to be positive. In today's organisations it is not the norm to have fun, to be happy or to be positive. Time and again, people allow themselves to be swept away in collective currents of negativity, despite the pain it causes. For example, a long-term employee of an organisation mired in the deficit discourse shared the following with dismay: 'I have ulcers because of this negative thinking and talking. Every day I come to work and I hear nothing but complaints, criticism and blaming. I hate coming to work.'

Often, people express that the appreciative approach works for them, in part because it gives people permission to feel positive and to be proud of their working experiences. The effect of the appreciative experience is so strong and powerful that it can even transform the deficit discourse and negative thinking. In the words of one employee: 'I am a very positive thinker, so this suits me very well. But I believe this process of appreciative inquiry is powerful enough to influence all of the staff – not just those of us who are already this way.'"[31]

## The wholeness principle

In a world that tends to separate, leading us to live in a constant duality, the wholeness principle holds that we are interconnected. We form part of a greater system. We live interconnected in a network of relationships. When we live and work taking all the system into account, our vision widens and we learn to flourish together. We particularly bring out the best of the system in its whole when we ask appreciative questions and hold generative conversations. By including stakeholders, relationships of relevance, those of the primary network and some of the secondary network, we stimulate creativity and build collective and personal capacity. We create a system of reciprocal support. We are applying social constructionism with the wholeness principle.

"In appreciative coaching we intentionally involve the social system of the client in order to support the desired results of the coaching. This permits us to use perspectives of a wide angle in involving others who are significant people and necessary relationships of the client, in conversations designed on purpose to:

- Go deeper into the client's appreciation of their essential achievements and contributions (Discover)
- Contribute to energising their dreams for the future and the future of the social system they belong to (Dreams)
- Give ideas in order to carry out actions aimed at the fulfilment of their dreams (Design)
- Actively give support in the phase of destiny and its development, forming the social architecture that will sustain the energy for the change (Destiny)."[32]

We could say that the system, in its wholeness, is wrapped in a flexible membrane that we define as we go along according to what we focus on in the coaching sessions. If we focus on a professional topic, we will include in the membrane the relevant relationships that the person has or should have in their job. If we focus on a personal topic that might have an influence on their family or friends, we will include those that we consider should be kept informed, those we should listen to, and those who can support the process.

Therefore, we should ask the question: Who, and maybe even what, is inside the membrane of the whole? We discover this as the sessions develop, according to who the necessary and significant people are, that bring or can bring value to the client's relational network. Including them allows us to appreciate different points of view, share dreams, and create a support network for the desired change. As Sloan and Canine (2007) say: "If we do not include in the coaching an interaction of the client with their network and their system, then it is not appreciative inquiry coaching."

When you live through a process of change you are crossing between three worlds, the one you know, the space in between with a foot either side, one foot in each paradigm, and the place or space you are aiming for. Perhaps you still don't know what this is, given that although you can glimpse it, you haven't fully lived it. In the coaching sessions, we encourage you to inform your friends, family or the team you work with, and for them to participate in some way or another in what is happening. In this way they feel included, offering you clarity with their multiple perspectives, and support with their presence and conversations.

Appreciative inquiry provides the context for people to feel free to act in a supported way. To act while feeling oneself to be supported is the quintessence of positive interdependence. When someone knows that other people recognise them and care about their work and are keen to cooperate, they feel secure to experiment, innovate and learn. In other words, the support of the system stimulates people to take on challenges and commit themselves to shared acts that bring out the best in them and their work.

# 15. Questions[33]

Questions mobilise our worlds.

> You can tell a person is clever by his answers. You can tell a person is wise by his questions.
> – Naguib Mahfouz, Nobel Prize for Literature

We are educated to look for answers, not to ask questions, which means that we tend to offer answers instead of questions. However, questions open up our perspective, they broaden our horizons and they allow us to look into things in order to deepen our understanding. Albert Einstein expressed it wisely: "If I had an hour to resolve a problem and my life depended on the solution, I would devote the first 55 minutes to finding the right question. Once I knew the correct question, I would be able to solve the problem in five minutes."

In the process of intervention with appreciative inquiry, the type of questions we formulate play an important role. We observe the principle of simultaneity, in which change begins to take place at the moment we ask the question. When we research and interview human groups, significant changes take place in people as a result of the questions. The interview with inquiry and change take place simultaneously. This is one of the strong points of appreciative inquiry.

The initial questions in a session of appreciative coaching create the atmosphere that can affect the entire process. The more positive the question, the greater and longer lasting the change. The way we formulate the questions has a big impact. The conversations, and the reality that arises out of them, will be marked by our questions. The efficiency of the actions that we undertake will depend on the quality of our questions. The ones that open the door to dialogue and discovery are an invitation to creativity and progressive thinking.

"The research shows one common denominator," explain Cooperrider *et al.* (2001). "After interviewing 100 of the most successful and happy people they could find, researchers were confused in the beginning. At first blush, there was nothing in common – certainly not education or socio-economic background. Finally, they found that each and every one of the 100 people had a special capability: to look for and find what was good in themselves, in others and all the situations in life. Because of their never-ending search for the positive, the good, the better, and the possible – and because of the ability to see and amplify the best in people and situations around them – these leaders were successful. People wanted to be around them. Those same people felt valued and understood. Strengths were elevated. Weaknesses became irrelevant.

They were experts at deliberately noticing, anticipating, and magnifying positive potential. And for our purposes here, one lesson stands out above all others:

If you truly wish to change your world, you must change your way of asking questions. It could be that the moment you do so, a totally different world will take shape around you."[34]

## Generative questions

> A paradigm shift occurs when a question is asked inside the current paradigm that can only be answered from outside it.
> – Marilee Goldberg (1997)

Questions can generate creative ideas that foster the right change. The art of asking ourselves questions has important implications, not only for changing our assumptions, but also in the creation of new possibilities for constructive action.

In general, appreciative inquiry coaching is begun with questions that lead people to focus on an optimum personal experience. This does not assure success, nor is it always enough to achieve the results sought after. Sometimes it is necessary to introduce questions that are the generators of new ideas and can lead us to a better reality. Gervase Bushe sets out four qualities of generative questions: "1. They are surprising; 2. They touch people's heart and spirit; 3. Talking about and listening to these stories and answers will build relationships; and 4. The questions force us to view reality a little differently, either because of how they ask us to think, or because of who we are listening to."[35]

The questions invite us to discover aspects of reality that were previously ignored or unknown; they lead us to suffer or to learn, to blame or take responsibility, to be aware or to stay anaesthetised. "A question not asked is a door not opened," says Marilee Goldberg.

The appreciative question does not reiterate the problem, but rather transcends it. It is a question that:

- Generates curiosity in the client.
- Stimulates reflective conversation.
- Brings underlying assumptions to the surface.
- Invites creativity and new possibilities.
- Opens the door to change.
- Generates energy, vitality and advancement.
- Channels the attention and focus of the chosen subject.
- Centres the intention.
- Touches the depth, the why and the what for of what you do and are.
- Connects to meaning.
- Leads us to the future.
- Evokes more questions.

Asking ourselves, for example: What can we do that might help us change this situation? What possibilities do we have that we haven't yet thought of? What small change can bring about the greatest impact? What solution would benefit us both? What moves and harmonises human relationships? The way of perceiving and understanding a situation can change in an unsuspected way and it can be approached from a new angle. It can improve our emotional bonds and our work relationships. They are questions that lead us to a constructive reflection. They arise from an appreciative perspective and stimulate appreciative dialogue. Appreciative inquiry is based on formulating questions that facilitate motivation, cooperation and the co-creation of a better reality.

Contrarily, the following questions anchor us in negativity and reiterate the problem: What is the biggest problem here? Why did I have to be born into such a problematic family? Why are you so often wrong? Why do we still have these problems?

The questions lead us either to stay stuck in the past, to live and learn in the present, or to generate transformation. There are questions that are incentives to transform, for example: What's the point of being trapped by stress, bitter feelings, in a void, and without achievements? How can I move on? Why am I going to carry on with these recurring experiences, which repeat themselves time and again? Why isn't my life going as I want it to? These questions invite us to review our internal programming and the perceptions, beliefs and memories that block our progress.

## How to find the right question?

To formulate powerful questions, it is important to become aware of assumptions and use them correctly. Vogt, Brown and Isaacs (2003) put this example, contrasting the question: "What did we do wrong and who is responsible?" with: "What can we learn from what has happened, and what possibilities do we see?" The first question assumes error and blame, and the person who has to answer it will without doubt go on the defensive. The second question encourages reflection, stimulates learning and collaboration among those involved.

As a coach, I should pay attention to my assumptions and put them to one side so they do not influence the construction of my questions. However, in appreciative coaching we do set out from some assumptions. For example, one is the assumption that people have a positive core, an essence which nurtures their peak experiences and gives them life. And through the questions we discover the essence, foster it and make it flourish. In any case, we do not always find the right question with a process of analysis and deduction; sometimes we need to be quiet.

In silence, meditating and relaxing the mind, the circuits of our brain calm down and we rest on our capacity to invent and to reinvent ourselves. In that space, we increase our creative capacity and the right question appears, allowing us to find the answer we need. To achieve this it is good to follow Anthony Strano's advice:

> Learn to ask questions and let go of wanting answers.
> When I am too focussed on answers, I lose them.
> Relevant questions are like brooms
> that sweep the mind and create a clean space.
> The mind needs clean space.
> Answers enter clean space.[36]

Feel curiosity for what happens inside you and what surrounds you. Don't blindly accept the answers that arise from your automatic pilot. Look for your inner truth and what is authentic on the outside, so as not to be taken in by mirages. Not all that glitters is gold. Ask.

## Guidelines for designing appreciative, powerful and generative questions

Appreciative inquiry questions have these characteristics:

**They are asked in an affirmative tone.** We don't look for what isn't going well, but rather what works and what one wants. They are questions that use words with positive feelings.

**They are constructed on a positive half-assumption.** For example, if we ask, "How are you?" it is a neutral question. However, if the question is: "What inspires you today?" it is a question in which there is a half-supposition that something inspires you. With the question I ask, I invite you to discover it, to think about it. And if nothing inspires you today, the question will in any case stay in your mind and you will look for the inspiration in the next hours or days. I will ask again tomorrow.

**They define broadly.** They allow for a wide definition of the topic. We don't limit ourselves to dealing with a situation from a microscopic perspective, but rather we define the topic so that it gives room to the system, as we explained in social constructionism (page 64). Broad topics open up the possibility of liberating conversations, with their dreams and longings on the horizon. That is, they offer an invitation that is expansive, open and inclusive.

**They value what is.** This encourages the appreciative imagination, helping the person to locate the experiences worth valuing. They highlight the possibilities of telling stories and narrating them. They find energising stories. When the person narrates a story that gives them life, they feel those positive emotions again, and connect to the images that give them hope and confidence. Our active listening while they narrate is very important. The person feels recognised and valued.

They go beyond the shared field and **raise the conversation** to a higher level. That is, if the conversation is centred on a situation put forward by the client, our question takes them beyond the place they are narrating from, opening them to other possibilities and broadening their perspective.

They respect unconditionally. They transmit **positive unconditional respect**. The person being asked the question does not feel threatened, insulted or attacked. They feel the genuine interest of our question.

**They evoke essential values**, aspirations and inspirations. The questions connect people to their essence, and their values, such as peace and love. See more on this subject in the section "Residing in your being", page 16.

They are powerful questions because:

- They generate a sense of belonging and opening.
- They are questions that are answers.
- They open up new perspectives.
- They incite a continuous re-questioning.
- They lead to the practice of active listening and being one hundred per cent present.
- They make you forget to be the expert, the one who always provides the answers.
- They generate motivation and empathy.
- They facilitate consensus.
- They open up the field of curiosity.
- They invite exploration and silence.

We can see the difference between appreciative questions and other kinds of questions by considering some typical questions in traditional problem solving, which focus on looking more deeply into the problem and its causes, for example:

Tell me, what is the problem?

What is it that doesn't work?
What is worrying you?
What do you need help with?
What is upsetting you?
What works?
What will you do about…?
What do you think made this happen?

Let us see what the questions in appreciative inquiry coaching are like:

What gives you energy?
What do you most value about yourself?
What is it that you most want?
What worked well before?
What works well now?
What is it that first attracted you to…?
What did you do to contribute to…?
How do you see yourself when you…?
How do you want to keep going forward by and for yourself?
If your worries were solved, how would you feel? What would be happening?
What would you do? How can you contribute to this ideal situation occurring?
What conversations should you propose and with whom?

# 16. Generative processes

In appreciative inquiry coaching we enter into a generative process. Generative means it generates a different reality to that of the starting point. It generates a desired reality, creating the necessary conditions to go towards it. For this, the coach should involve the client in the conversation on the positive present and future, and focus on it, instead of dealing with the problems of the past and present.

Talking about problems wears you out, minimising and exhausting the energy necessary for change and living the life one wants to live. Instead of inquiring into the causes of your problems, we inquire into the causes of your successes and your moments of wholeness. That way, we connect you to inspiration and awaken your motivation to go forward. With generative process we begin the push towards a longed for reality; we inquire into strengths and the positive core; we imagine and we innovate. As I already explained in chapter 4, in accepting suffering, it is not a question of denying problems and the emotions they cause. It is rather about asking questions which lead to life-giving conversations where, instead of wallowing, one connects to their inner power, in order to dominate the dragons, like Saint George.

The generative processes in appreciative inquiry coaching try to "enable people in organizations to become more aware of their own strengths and abilities in ways that increase their effectiveness in all parts of their life and to create robust support for change in the client's social system."[37]

We could determine five generative processes, summarised as:

- Creating and maintaining a positive approach, that is, choosing the positive and the appreciative stance as the focus of the inquiry.

- Narrating stories of life experiences. It is the process that inquires into stories that are life-giving forces.
- Locating subjects that appear in the stories and selecting topics in order to inquire more deeply into the accompanying process.
- Creating shared images for a desired future.
- Finding innovative ways to propitiate that future.

The generative process can also take place through five phases which incorporate the five processes mentioned above. Let us see them.

Appreciative inquiry is made concrete in a process of five phases. They are like a constellation of five stars. Each phase lights up new aspects of the positive core (page 11), like a star, and the capacities of people who, on relating to each other in an appreciative way, increase their strengths, their imagination and their creative capacity to innovate. Each phase has the name of the main activity that they are made up of: Define, Discover, Dream, Design and Destiny, as we see in this diagram:

These phases are known as the 5Ds.

In the following we will explore the way the 5Ds are applied in coaching sessions.

## Define

In this first stage we choose what topic or topics we will focus on in our coaching sessions. In appreciative inquiry (AI) coaching we specify topics, subjects, lines along which we wish to work, and we don't tend to use the word objectives. Using the terminology of fixing objectives has its origin in military strategy. In our sessions we focus on topics to explore, inquire into and discover. In this first conversation it is important to establish a positive connection between coach and client.

To do so, we inquire into stories (personal or of the team) that are life-giving, that connect to the positive core (page 11), telling us about peak experiences, moments of wholeness, complicity, success, collaboration; what the person has enjoyed living and wants to live more of.

To define the topics that we are going to focus the coaching on, we ask and listen to the person narrate their situation and what they want. We soon realise that in general they use a discourse of deficit; that is, they focus on what they don't want, what they don't have, what isn't going well, what they don't like, what they don't do well, etc. I don't let them continue with this discourse for more than ten minutes; I ask permission to interrupt and I say:

> What would your ideal be?
> If all this that doesn't work were resolved, what would be happening?
> When things went well, what worked? What did you bring to the situation?
> What would you like to happen?

With this kind of question I change the direction of the discourse and the conversation. It turns towards what the person wants and what moves them, motivates and is life-giving to them.

To get to know the client and find the best questions and the topics to go deeper into, we can explore their vision of the world. This covers the person's beliefs and values. It is about asking them questions in order to reveal, bring to the light, how they see themselves in the world. Do they see themselves as a victim or centred in their personal core? Do they see themselves as useful or useless? Do they see themselves as insignificant? How much do they value their contribution to the world? When asking these questions we are careful about the language we use.

From the first coaching session, we use appreciative language. We introduce words relating to affirmations, images, dreams and potential that lead in a generative direction. We reformulate in the affirmative and appreciative certain phrases that the client says to us when they use a language of deficit. For example, if they say to me: "I am tired of trying and they still don't listen to me," I ask: "When did they listen to you? What was happening in the relationship at that moment?" With the question I lead them to visualise moments in which they have been listened to and then I inquire into those images, evoking what it is that makes the listening easier. We inquire into that and not their tiredness. We see what makes listening possible, and what dynamics create it. Doing so, they find new hopes and the tiredness diminishes.

It is also important to understand what clients bring in terms of personal work, that is, their levels of experience and ability in the area of self-analysis and self-discovery. Sometimes they have already been through a therapeutic or coaching process and are looking for something different, more positive and generative. It is good to find out what worked for them on that process, and what has attracted them to start coaching sessions that are appreciative. What they are looking for and whether they are prepared to commit themselves to it.

To know the client better, help them connect to their positive core and enter into appreciative language, we can ask some of the following questions. They can be proposed as questions at the beginning of the coaching process, almost like an interview in order to gather information and experiences from the client. Most of the questions that follow are taken from the book of Orem et al. (2007)[38] and adapted for this text.

### *Your story*

Describe your three greatest accomplishments to date.

What made these accomplishments stand out for you?

What have you incorporated into your current actions from your past accomplishments?

How could you use what you have learned from these accomplishments to assist you in making future changes?

What major transitions have you gone through in the past two years? (For example, new assignments, new residence, new relationship, new job, etc.)

If you have worked with a coach previously, or in a similar one to one relationship, for example, with a tennis coach, a therapist, a private piano teacher, what worked well for you in that relationship? What worked in that job?

If you have worked with a coach, and you are not currently doing so, how did that relationship end?

What works well in your life now?

What is it that first attracted you to…?

### *Your life*

What are the five most positive aspects in your life?

What five aspects would you like to change in your life that would make it even more satisfying, whole, effective and joyful?

In what way do you want to move on? How do you want to keep going forward for and by yourself?

Who are the key supportive people in your life, and what do they provide for you?

On a scale of 1 to 10 (1 being the least effective and 10 the most effective), rate the quality of your life? By what criteria did you rate yourself?

What percentage of the life you are leading is actually YOUR life?

### *Your self today*

List five adjectives or values that describe you at your best.

What prevents you from being at your best and being the best version of yourself?

What activates you and gets you going?

What energises you?

What do you most value about yourself?

What saps your energy?

What are you learning and accepting about yourself at present?

In what ways do you currently spend time, which, if you were to spend it differently, would yield greater achievements and happiness?

What do you consume at present that, if you didn't, would allow you to be healthier (for example, alcohol, caffeine, sugar, etc.)?

When you are in your best shape, living your potential, shining from the best of your being, how do you see yourself?

Could therapy resolve some issue effectively in your life now?

### *Your potential*

What is your personal and/or professional vision of yourself?

What would you like to contribute to the world?

What do you most wish to achieve in the next three years?

How ready are you to go for it?

What is it that you most want?

### *Make it happen*

Why have you sought out a coach?

What are three immediate changes you can make to get you off to a good start in our coaching?

How can I help you to be more effective in working towards your goals?

What approaches to change have you found most effective for you?

What responsibility do you have for ensuring that our relationship works well?

How will you know that your coaching experience has been effective?

Other questions that we can ask are:

- Remember a moment of wholeness, a moment you would highlight because you felt abundant, complete and whole. You were shining with all your potential. Your being was blossoming with what is in you.
  How did you experience that moment? How did you feel? What made it special? What were you radiating?

- If you were to project that state of wholeness into the future, how does that experience connect to your dreams and to what you most long to be and live in your life?

- Of what you are, what quality, virtue and characteristic of yours would you like to nurture and have more of?
  When you achieve it, how will that experience benefit your environment and your close relationships?

Of all the subjects that have arisen in the answers, and in the stories that have emerged, we are going to give priority to what most matters for now, and for the next months. We enter into discovering and inquiring into what the client most wants or needs, in the framework of the ideas that have come up. It is important that the subject attracts them, and that they want to explore it. If the client finds the topic boring or an obligation, feeling that they have to work on it out of duty, but are not enthused by it, then we haven't chosen the subject well. It has to motivate them and they should feel curiosity about inquiring into how to go about it.

Xavier came to see me to begin a coaching process just after Easter. I asked him how his holidays had gone and he told me he had attended a workshop on how to be a clown. He had wanted to be a clown since he was a child, but his family did not support him in it. Now, in his forties, he was learning to be what he had always been attracted to being. He came with the idea of working on tolerance towards his boss in the coaching sessions. Xavier works for an insurance broker. He had read my book: *Dare to Live,* in which I embark on a reflection on the importance of tolerance for maintaining healthy relationships.

Xavier got very upset with his boss. When he was with him, it brought out the worst of him. He felt the need to be tolerant in order to put up with his working relationship. I asked him if he saw himself being tolerant; he answered that he didn't. I asked him if he was attracted to working on tolerance, his answer was a resounding no. It was clear that this was not the topic to choose for our coaching sessions.

Continuing in search of a subject, I asked him various questions, out of which a list of topics arose, for example, working on being more loving, kinder and more communicative. But on inquiring a little more into each of the topics, it was clear that we weren't on the right path, because they didn't carry enough weight to be able to generate attractor images of the future. Xavier didn't see himself being more loving at work, and nor did he feel like being kinder to his boss.

It occurred to me to inquire into his longing to be a clown.

There, we hit the nail on the head. He was very attracted to being able to incorporate elements of being a clown into his working environment, and into his life in general. So we began to uncover stories of when Xavier had most been a clown, what made it easy for him to make people laugh, how he managed not to let others influence him, and how he was able to change the mood of the people around him. We realised that a clown makes people laugh by being loving, nice, tolerant and kind. The qualities that he wanted to work on as an obligation we could now work on out of excitement. As you see, the chosen subject is much wider than the proposed topic of his relationship with his boss. It is a subject that will benefit different areas of Xavier's life and allow him to incorporate more excitement and meaning into his life.

Let's go on to the next phase: Discovery.

## Discovery

The way in which we perceive reality is conditioned by our conversations, and defines what we see and what we don't see. In the Discovery phase, we broaden our perspective in order to find the positive core that has made us vibrate and given us strength to move forward. What we have resorted to when we overcame challenges or went through important changes. We refer to what we could call our vital essence.

As we saw in the narrative principle, the stories we tell ourselves over and over again create and perpetuate the reality of our perceptions. These stories have the power to limit our options, as well as expand the possibilities we can imagine and create.

In this phase we inquire into stories connected to the subject or subjects chosen in the defining phase, emphasising what was life-giving, what was motivating, connecting them to their wholeness, opening them and revealing some important aspect.

On inquiring appreciatively into stories that the client tells us, we help them to revisit their own story with other eyes, to relive experiences that have nourished them and to reconnect to their strengths, thanks to which they have moved forward.

The focus of the coach in this phase is:

- To lead the client to a perspective that empowers them.
- To affirm the sensation of what is possible.
- To cultivate and support the client in creating a positive and hopeful future in which they see their wishes fulfilled, first rooting it in the best of their past.
- To support reflection and observation.

We use the narrative principle, aware that stories transform. We apply the poetic principle to recognise and value multiple realities. And from the beginning we involve the relational system of the person, so that they experience social constructionism and the wholeness principle, thus bringing into the conversations multiple points of view with a wide reach.

Going on with the example of Xavier, the topic we defined was to live being more of a clown. In the Discovery phase, we were inquiring into the peak moments of his life, when he felt that his clown qualities emerged. This enabled us to uncover his positive core and see what strengths were lying inside him that made it easy for him to bring about laughter, laugh himself and have a good time with others. We saw moments in which he was capable of generating laughter and well-being in his job. On telling me his stories as someone capable of making others laugh, he made me laugh. And soon, the moment arrived when, for example, he rang me at some point, be it to make an appointment or change it for another day, and we were instantly laughing. He began to express it with me and this strengthened his confidence in his own capacity.

## Dream

We often find that we aspire to ideals that are not ours; rather they have been injected into us by our parents, our educators or society. We chase success in order to be someone. What is it we are really longing for? In this phase we are going to discover the client's longings, what they want, and are attracted to. We create attractive images that motivate them to go forward to their desired future. On discovering their dreams and aspirations, the emotional positive attractor is activated, which activates the stimulation of the parasympathetic system, benefiting the person by improving their general health, and lowering blood pressure (Insel, 1997; Sapolsky, 2004).[39]

The focus of the coach in the dream phase consists of:

- Encouraging the client to create images of possibilities.
- Inviting the client to give a voice to their desired future.
- Facilitating the appearance of images that will act as guides in moving towards the desired future.
- Affirming the dream or dreams of the client.

This is important, since what usually happens is that someone hasn't given voice to their dreams out of fear of people's rejection, and because they do not want to be excluded from their relational system. The fear of rejection makes us renounce our dreams. When the coach affirms the client's dreams, they are empowering them to feel good about themselves and their longings, and to dare to create the conditions enabling them to follow the path towards living their desired future.

In the session we can do a visualisation. Let's look at an example, using the topic of Xavier that we saw in the Define phase. I invite Xavier to sit down comfortably and relax, closing his eyes. After making him breathe deeply a few times, I say to him:

We make a trip in time, three years have passed, and you are living out one of your passions; you feel you have been able to become the clown that you always longed to be. Your inner clown expresses itself in a lively way. You are living what you most desire to live. You are brimming over and feeling whole. You go to your work and you are radiant. You light up the faces of the people around you with smiles.

How do you feel?

What is happening?

What have you done to get here?

What do you do that is different?

Who is with you?

What is the place like?

What way does being a clown impact positively in the world that surrounds you?

What else do you see? Is there any other aspect that you see and want to share?

We do the visualisation after a brief relaxation, in which the person feels comfortable and breathes consciously. After the Discovery phase, we now know what it is that allows the client to connect to their positive core. Now we connect them to their core, and, led by that energy of their essence, they can imagine a future that inspires and calls them. It is a question of reviving their inner calling. Once we have led the client to visualise their future, we ask questions one by one, leaving a space for them to respond. They can also answer out loud. Sometimes we may even ask them to make a graphic of their image. We make a note of the essential elements that are appearing. We will work with these elements in the next phase, the Design phase.

In Xavier's dream various essential elements emerged, which we grouped as:

- Detachment; he wasn't influenced by others, but rather,

thanks to that lightness and healthy distance, Xavier was able to make them laugh, remaining in his positive centre.

- He laughed more and increased his sense of humour.
- He dared to begin breakthrough conversations, that is, they broke the ice, the dryness and seriousness.
- He was able to put things in context and not be overwhelmed by problems. He maintained a broad vision that enabled him to relativize situations.

With these elements we see that in the sessions we went much further than the initial situation we looked at: of not being influenced by his boss. Now, Xavier is looking at all his relational environment and how his change of attitude and presence improves his state of mind and his surroundings. This is what usually happens in appreciative inquiry coaching sessions. The client comes with an initial subject that is narrow in scope, but quickly the topic is broadened, connecting it to their vital core and making them flourish in all the spheres of their life.

We take these areas or subjects to the next stage, Design, in which we will design proposals of possibilities.

## Design

In this phase, the coach focuses on accompanying the client in staying focused on their dreams, and on what takes priority, what they most want and the essential. It is about affirming the reality of their dream and supporting conscious choices and actions, in full awareness, which will facilitate it. We design proposals as principles to be put into action.

We review all the elements that appeared in the visualisation of the dream. We group the ideas into subjects that are key to making the dream reality. They will be subjects that we will work on to design proposals to bring about the desired changes. We put into words a future that inspires, and is, at the same time, rooted in the best experiences of the past.

In Xavier's case, taking into account the four main areas that arose from the dream, we saw that he needed to establish proposals for action aimed at:

- Keeping a healthy distance, being an observer, detached.
- Cultivating his sense of humour.
- Being more daring and letting go.
- Broadening his vision.

We worked on the essential elements for him to be able to apply and live out these four issues. And Xavier created some proposals, sentences that are like mottos, written in the affirmative, in the positive, expressing the vision of what he wants, not what he doesn't want.

The proposals designed in this phase are provocative and imply affirmations of what is possible. They are declarations or affirmations indicating what one wants and how one wants it. They imply an affirmation or declaration that links the best of 'what is' with 'what could be'.

Let's look at some criteria for creating some good provocative proposals. A proposal is provocative when:

- It broadens the limits of the *status quo*.
- It questions assumptions or common routines.
- It is based on what has worked in the past.
- It transmits positive images (the *Dream* phase) of the desired future.

It is provocative in the way that it forces the limits of the *status quo*, it questions what is taken for granted, and daily routines, and helps to suggest desired possibilities for the person and the people around them.

We can ask questions that help the client to think beyond the already established. For example, I asked Xavier: Supposing that anything that we imagine is possible in relation to your sense of humour, how could you live it in your working environment? Supposing you can imagine being totally daring and letting go completely, what would be happening in your life? With the answers, we opened up the path to the provocative proposals. They are provocative for him. What widens the limits for one person and brings about change for them may not work for another. Therefore, the person who evaluates whether it is provocative or not is the client themselves.

Some of the proposals and declarations that Xavier formulated were:

- When I receive serious looks I smile.
- I allow myself to have fun at work.
- I go into work wearing the invisible clown suit.
- When I dress in the morning, metaphorically I put the clown suit on top of my suit and tie.
- I dare to say what I think.
- I breathe and smile before responding to criticism.

The proposals are written in the present tense. They express clearly and strongly the image of how things will be when the positive core is fully materialised in all their actions, strategies, processes, systems, decisions and collaborations. In this way, the provocative proposals redirect their daily activities and generate future possibilities. They mark a vision that the person and the members of their system share. It is important that the design fully integrate 'the best of the past and of the possible', and is consistent with the result the client wants to achieve. In sum, the provocative proposals offer a clear and shared vision of the destiny that the person wants.

### Destiny

Up to this point we have defined a topic or various to inquire into, we have gone into a discovery of the best experiences and peak moments related to the subject, and we have created a dream, which has been given shape in provocative proposals or affirmations of possibility. Throughout the process we have left to one side the typical jargon of problem solving; we have focused on locating the sources of energy and vitality, trusting they will give us strength to deal with the problems that we might have.

In this phase, the coach focuses on helping the client to recognise their dreams in the present. It is a question of grounding them. Of seeing what aspects of their longings they can begin to make real, what first steps they can and want to take, and who they are going to involve. The coach facilitates and makes it easier for the client to expand their ability to convert their dreams into reality. It is about supporting the client in keeping faith and trusting when the road is tough. We are going to design actions to turn them into destiny. We can also ask questions that encourage them to reflect on how the progress will be measured.

It is important to pay attention in order not to fall into the known and common space of problem resolution. Without realising, we can fall into analysing the problem, planning change and, finally, looking for the necessary treatment and actions to carry out the plan. We can easily enter the terrain that we know so well: analysing what we find, planning what we dream and acting on destiny. In so doing, we lose the unique contributions that the appreciative inquiry perspective offers us in the face of change.

In the traditional model of problem solving, two phases can be seen: in the first we analyse and we plan, and in the second, we act based on the plan, with the idea of creating a bridge between the situation we find ourselves in and the one we want to be in.

In the appreciative inquiry perspective, the perception is

different. We don't have to create any bridge, or action plan. We are creating, through dialogue, language and evoking images, a new and inspiring future, and we generate actions out of that vision of the future. The actions don't arise out of what doesn't work, but rather out of the attractive vision of the future, with us rooted in our positive core.

In the example of Xavier, he doesn't plan to have more of a sense of humour in order to get over his anger and his intolerance. Rather, he incorporates the sense of humour as part of his longing to be a clown.

Once the client connects to their positive core and declares a possible new future as a provocative proposal, they are already influencing and creating that future. We keep the future alive, connected to the central, life-giving values. We do so by asking questions which evoke an appreciative flow. These questions are already an action plan. Asking oneself these questions is the expression of destiny, since it implies an ongoing commitment to the three aspects of the appreciative approach: continuity, transition and innovation.

Another three aspects of the appreciative flow are three areas of inquiry: the best experience, values and wishes. Luke Younge[40] explains them as follows:

The best experience inquiry asks questions like:

- Where is this possibility already happening?
  So there is no pressure to invent only new actions – in fact there will always be some actions that already exist that are creating this new future. By treating the possibility as a microcosm of the whole process we tap into a huge source of energy and find the process continues to carry us. Immediately it should be clear that the subtle pressure to invent new actions is off – we start as we always do in the appreciative approach with where things are already

working.

- The values inquiry asks questions such as:
  What made this life-giving experience significant for you? At any time we need to we can begin to mine these actions for further refinement of and connection to the positive core.

- The wishes inquiry asks questions like:
  Where does this possibility have the biggest potential to impact you?

Within cultivation of an authentic appreciation for self and others, we can ask the client to stretch themselves by looking at areas that benefit most from being brought into connection with the positive core they have identified for themselves. This inquiry will always keep the leverage high – *minimal effort for maximal results*. When things begin feeling like hard work, struggle and effort, it is a clue that there is a disconnect from the positive core. It's not that there isn't hard work, there certainly is; it is simply that this hard work is *not resisted*. When there's no resistance the task is simply the task and is not felt as struggle and effort.

The energy flows.

## The process in the phases of the 5Ds

Appreciative inquiry coaching implies a change of paradigm: from deficit-based and lack, to one that is strength-based. It is a fluid and non-linear process, although on seeing the phases, we might think that we go from discovering to dreaming, from designing to destiny. It isn't linear; rather it is flexible and the Ds can be applied when and how it is necessary in any order that is appropriate for the moment.

We are not going from the present problem to the future

solution. We are not creating bridges between what doesn't work and what will work. Rather, we connect to our positive core of energy out of which we act with a high level of creativity and improvisation. The change begins here and now in the moment we ask the question and connect to our strengths.

In the process of the coaching sessions, we can evaluate as we go along, using the three areas of inquiry that Younge sets out. In our questions, we use the approach of peak experiences, of the best experiences: "What worked best there? Where did your possibility – your topic – shine through this week? In the inquiry into values we ask: What made that success significant for you? How was that experience meaningful for you and for the people in your environment? And if we inquire into wishes: Where does your provocative proposition have the biggest potential impact now? Who can it have a bigger impact on? What area do you think is ripe now?"[41]

# 17. What features make appreciative inquiry coaching different?

Appreciative inquiry coaching is effective for multiple purposes, which are worked on in the processes and stages of the sessions. They might cover leadership, transition, personal and organisational development, the search for meaning and other wishes that someone looks to the professional help of a coach for.

Appreciative inquiry coaching is not the only one to incorporate the belief that the client has the ability to recreate themselves. Neither is it unique in incorporating a change of language in order to achieve the established objectives. But both aspects, the first connected to the constructionist principle, and the second to the principle of simultaneity, are present in all appreciative inquiry (AI) coaching practice.

Something unique in AI coaching is that it focuses primordially on a change of language. We use a language that connects us to our guiding images, to what we want and a language of abundance. A language that evokes positive emotions, appreciative thought, and generative conversations. It is the language that we use in the stories and the appreciative questions we ask. See more on the language of abundance in chapter 8.

AI coaching also differentiates itself from other approaches in coaching in its set of fundamental principles of appreciative inquiry. These principles strengthen, enrich and differentiate AI coaching from other approaches. We apply the constructionist principle which is inclusive, that is, this and that, instead of this or that. Supported by the constructionist and poetic principles, we dance between the different possible perspectives and the principle of wholeness; all the system is taken on board. As well as these three principles, we base ourselves on the ten principles that I have described in chapter 14.

It is a way of coaching that focuses on strengths. The

strengths experienced in my personal history empower me to achieve the future I long for. Looking for my guiding images and focusing on them, I stimulate the positive emotional attractor and the parasympathetic nervous system. This stimulates the glands in the endocrine system which produce many benefits for physical, mental and emotional health. One highlighted aspect of the AI coaching process is that, on stimulating the positive emotional attractor more than the negative one, the impact is significant, for both the health and well-being of the person. With this stimulus it is easier for the desired change to be sustained.

"However, the coaching that focuses on deficiencies awakens the sympathetic nervous system which is activated when the body goes into fight or flight mode. It is the response of the body to stress," says Boyatzis. "When through coaching by deficiencies the negative emotional attractor is stimulated, this causes the person to go on the defensive, awakening the neuro-endocrine systems characteristic of the human response to stress and the reduction in cognitive, perceptual and immune functioning. Coaching by achievement awakens the negative emotional attractor in the client on focusing on their weaknesses and deficiencies. The negative feelings that this approach awakens generate a defensive attitude, of threat and blame which awaken the sympathetic nervous system."[42]

"Negative emotions can overwhelm the positive ones if these are not fostered. The mention of a weakness could awaken a response of the negative emotional attractor in the person. If the client is pressurised, or even if they are encouraged to make the changes desired by the organisation or by the system they live in, or by the coach themselves, and they are not what the client wants, the 'should be' and the 'I have to' are awakened, and this raises the heartbeat, the blood pressure and the breathing rate. The effect of this in the brain is that the blood flows to the neural circuits that are considered necessary for survival and it lessens the access to other neural circuits, for example, the immune system. The activation of the sympathetic nervous system is related to emotions such as fear, anger, anxiety and feeling depressed" (De Quattro and Feng, 2002).[43]

It is not that those emotions are stimulated on purpose, but that, on holding a conversation focused on what doesn't work, on what one is afraid of or what one doesn't like, the images and associations associated with it are increased. When, for example, you tell a story about what makes you afraid or angry, you see it, you feel it again, you use a language that evokes it and that way you nurture it. So as not to encourage this in happening, we stimulate conversations that awaken positive feeling, bearing in mind that: "The contagious effect of the emotions expands to others around it (Barsade and Gibson, 2007) and even contributes to creating a climate or state of mind in relationships, teams and organisations."[44]

Sloan and Canine (2007) state that "it is our conviction that the appreciative inquiry philosophy and practice is in and of itself the ideal process for both enabling people in organisations to become more aware of their own strengths and abilities in ways that increase their effectiveness in all parts of their life, and to create robust support for change in the client's social system."

The framework of social constructionism that AI coaching moves within helps people to think about how they would like their world to be, and to explore how the positive can contribute to its development, in a different way to how it is dealt with in other coaching methodologies. Unlike other coaching, in the appreciative inquiry model the client is involved together with their relevant relational, professional and social system. Their system is included.

The appreciative inquiry coach is aware that the client is not alone, and that for the fulfilment of their dreams, they should take into account their relational network and their social system. To do so, they incorporate into the coaching session the awareness of the impact that the person has on their system, and the impact the system has on them. They look for what gives life to the system and how the client contributes to revitalizing it. And they discover what it is that gives life to the client from their system; how it can be more nurtured and inspired, turning it into a healthy system.

Appreciative inquiry offers a structure that makes it easier to live in a dynamic that mobilises the necessary energy to act, considering and applying the collective agreements. When this occurs, many problems are resolved.

In this relational sphere, we have already seen that AI coaching proposes a radical difference in the context of traditional coaching. Radical, because in the majority of agreements of traditional coaching, confidentiality is maintained in all the process between the coach and the client. When we look to involve others in the process, we are opening it to an exchange that stops being private, and that allows for a flow of conversations, meanings and actions between the client and their necessary relational network. It is the client that determines how much they want to open themselves and in which aspects, but the process invites participation, and therefore an openness and transparency with regards to what is being dealt with.

Let's consider some other differential aspects of appreciative coaching.

### *Generative processes*

In AI coaching one is aware that every process should connect the person to what gives them life. The sessions are focused on what is life-giving, lifts them, and connects them to their strengths. Thus, the person manages to come out of the sessions passionate, enthusiastic and open.

### *Positive core*

Every process of appreciative inquiry seeks to connect to the positive core, reinforcing it, enhancing and extending it. The positive core is the seed that turns into the sap that gives life to all living systems; it is the blood that circulates in the system of the body.

> The positive core is one of the biggest resources, albeit the least recognised, of the sphere of change management today.
> – David Cooperrider (page 11)

### *Change of language*

As we have seen in chapter 8, one of the main factors in appreciative inquiry is the usage of a language that favours the connection with positive emotions, with the attractor images of the future, with the memories that stimulate the expression of the positive core.

On focusing on problems, it is possible that it is difficult to think of possibilities beyond them. And, in those cases, it is rare for the client to be passionate and enthusiastic during the process. Instead, they feel obligation and duty, not motivation and excitement. Rather than talking about what is not going well, what there isn't, about what we don't like, we talk about what there is, what we want, what works.

### *Phases*

Appreciative inquiry coaching follows a dynamic of five phases. It is a '5D' cycle which moves like a spiral. It is not a linear process that begins with Define and ends with Destiny. It is a constellation in movement; as we advance, we discover new subjects to continue inquiring into. We create a new and inspiring future through dialogue, appreciative language and evoking images, and we generate actions out of that vision of the future. We are careful not to go into the terrain that we know so well, analysing what we discover, planning what we dream and acting on destiny.

### *Thinking Partner*

The thinking partner accompanies the person in order to bring out their exceptionality, their essentialness and their capacity, together with others, so that shared living with others is more manageable, and the person feels comfortable, able to be themselves in their relational system, and in their environment. It is about knowing how to sustain the field of the client, creating a state of alertness and a state of awareness. I develop this subject in chapter 21.

# 18. Coaching for leaders

## By Joep C. de Jong

### A new look at the concept of leadership

In our daily lives we find that we are dealing with leaders, with leadership, and with the concept of leading and following. Whilst we see spectacular technological changes in our world, in reality we only touch on the surface of what leadership and the concept of leadership mean in our changing era. The motive to affirm this lies in the fact that, not only are we discovering more about what leadership requires in a particular situation, but that as our environment continues to change, we also need to look again at how the concept of leadership is evolving. And it might well be that, in accordance with what people like Otto Scharmer (*Theory U*) and David Cooperrider (in his model of appreciative inquiry) say, we not only should look at what we can learn from the past, but we should also reflect on our journey when we take a look back from an imaginary position in the future. This last is pertinent when we consider the questions: "I want you to coach me in understanding 'appreciative leadership'?" or "Is it wise to coach that person on their journey to becoming an 'appreciative leader'?" Adopting this perspective of 'looking back from the future' adds a new dimension to the coaching of leaders.

What will appreciative leadership bring to this world? Can we coach people, managers and leaders so that they become appreciative leaders? Reflecting on these questions – this chapter only came into being after many conversations – we trust that we will be able to offer you some thoughts, some ideas, hopefully even some useful instruments in order to help you in your personal search for the answers to the questions that we ask.

However, let's begin by first giving a brief description, a brief definition of what we understand by an appreciative leader. We will not try to give a definitive answer to this question, but rather use some quotes from people who have been trying to define this concept. In his prologue to *Appreciative Leaders: In the Eye of the Beholder*,[45] David Cooperrider says, amongst other things, that: "Everything the appreciative leader does conveys to others a genuine, respect-filled, positive intention to produce enduring change for world benefit. Reality for the appreciative leader is not a given: It is there for our active shaping in the direction of higher purposes." In their book *Appreciative Leadership*,[46] Whitney, Trosten-Bloom and Rader use the following definition: "Appreciative leadership is the relational capacity to mobilise creative potential and turn it into positive power – to set in motion positive ripples of confidence, energy, enthusiasm and performance – to make a positive difference in the world."

From my personal experience, coaching a manager, a leader, in order to become an appreciative leader as described in the quotes, requires, from both the coach and the client, the understanding of the importance of concepts like experience, wisdom, integrity and even spirituality. To broaden your understanding of what and how an appreciative leader might be, I suggest reading the chapter of the same title in the book by Subirana and Cooperrider (2013).[47]

So the essential question that we want to deal with in this chapter is: Can you, as coach, apply what has been said in the previous chapters to help people to become aware of the importance of the appreciative approach and of the potential of people to become appreciative leaders? To do so we should understand first and foremost the fact that becoming an appreciative leader begins with the decision to take on a lifestyle. It is a way of seeing the world and relationships. It is broader than the mere fact of learning a set of values, norms and rules, a series of competences that can be learned as one learns a language or understands a balance sheet and a profit and loss account.

The understanding of the need to develop a way of being an

appreciative leader has to be present in both the coach and the client. Coaching people on the journey to developing their leadership is, in this sense, a huge challenge, when you as coach, involving the community, try to coach that person, the leader, for the next phase of development, really getting in touch with their talents, their aptitudes and their essence. One of the key questions that they should ask themselves in this phase will be: Why do they aspire to following this path of becoming an appreciative leader?

As explained in chapter 17, some of the differences between traditional coaching and appreciative inquiry coaching are: a) the participation of the community and the system in the coaching process; and b) looking for cases and experiences during which the client was performing at his best and looking for the values that support those cases and experiences.

For the coaches who want to work with people who aspire to achieving more appreciation in their style of administrating, managing and leading, we will focus on six spheres and provide some ideas, and guidance, on what and how it can be done. The first is inspiration, given that to be an appreciative leader, one should be inspired and inspire. As Whitney and Trosten-Bloom state,[48] "The courage of inspiration is to awaken the creative spirit. It is to inspire creativity, confidence and hope to innovate and create a better future."

## Inspiration

One of the questions which offers a great challenge in our work in appreciative coaching is: Can we inspire people in and through the process of coaching? Often, we don't believe this to be the task of a coach, not even an appreciative inquiry coach. Even so, I believe that the question is pertinent in the case of training someone to become an appreciative leader. What we should do in this sense is support the client so that they find their source of inspiration and, at the same time, keep an eye out for what I usually call the collective inspiration of the organisation.

Inspiration constitutes one of the first steps on the road to understanding our way of being. What is, in reality, the objective of you being here, doing what you are doing; what might the true spirit of who you are be? Understanding and being able to connect with their inspiration turns out to be key to this process. Coaches that try to give structure to the manager or leader on their path to understanding the concept of being an appreciative leader, and of coaching that person to 'manage by example', should be very aware of their key role in exploring those dimensions. They can ask them questions that make them aware of the impact of their actions and words, and the fact that, when they do not act as an example, their words lose force.

It is important that the coach understands that leaders go through a process whereby their journey takes them closer to the essence of who they really are. Why is this important? It is because the choices we make on our journey will in the end decide whether or not we will inspire others. Like many of us, managers and leaders face one of the basic questions of all humanity: Why are we on this planet? And, although we might not be aware of it, life is full of distractions that take us away from this fundamental question. In the case of managers and leaders, even more so.

From my personal experience, at the first lecture – back in the 1980s – at a well-known business management school, when they asked us: "Why are you here?" the answer was, ultimately: "For the dividends. To create shareholder value." Whilst it may be that nowadays most managers and leaders have a point of view that is a bit more progressive, it continues to be true for many of those who make up the business world, and it still is one of the main 'distractions' in my opinion. So, managers and leaders can, given their positions, face even more distractions in becoming who they really are than many other people in our society.

They have to balance different interests, and in that process they can lose sight of themselves; it is here where the coach plays a fundamental role. The task of asking: Are you doing what is of use to your greater (spiritual) journey? In organisations this is generally a journey that leads us from the declarations of vision and of mission – very much on the edges of any organisation – through the values of that organisation towards layers that can be defined as collective inspiration, followed by the objective and finally the essence or the soul of the individual.

See figure 2[49] which shows, in a simplified form, the importance of vision, mission and values in the old economy, where organisations are the most important elements with their shareholders being the most relevant people. The roots of the new economy lie in appreciating each person, their purpose and the understanding that honouring the relationship between us is key to success. In our societies both meet at a point that is referred to as collective inspiration. This meeting point happens when the vision, the mission and the values of the organisation align with the spirituality, the purpose and the values of the person. In figure 2 we see how the two triangles overlap, and it is in that space where the collective wisdom is found, giving space to the collective inspiration. When we work from that space, we feel commitment, enjoyment, respect, and the organisation we work for can be successful and serve as a great workplace. This happens when our personal journey is aligned with the journey undertaken by the organisation.

As coaches and clients we should be aware of the level we are conducting the coaching on. If we want to apply appreciative inquiry coaching, we should do so by looking at our organisations from the perspective of the new economy. The link between both economies, which allows us to remain connected to the models and principles of the old economy, is where we will find collective inspiration.

When you work with leaders from this perspective, it is good to think of possible questions such as: Give me an example where you see how inspiration made a difference in your organisation. What for you is the meaning of the inspiration? What importance does it have? Give me an example of when you were inspired.

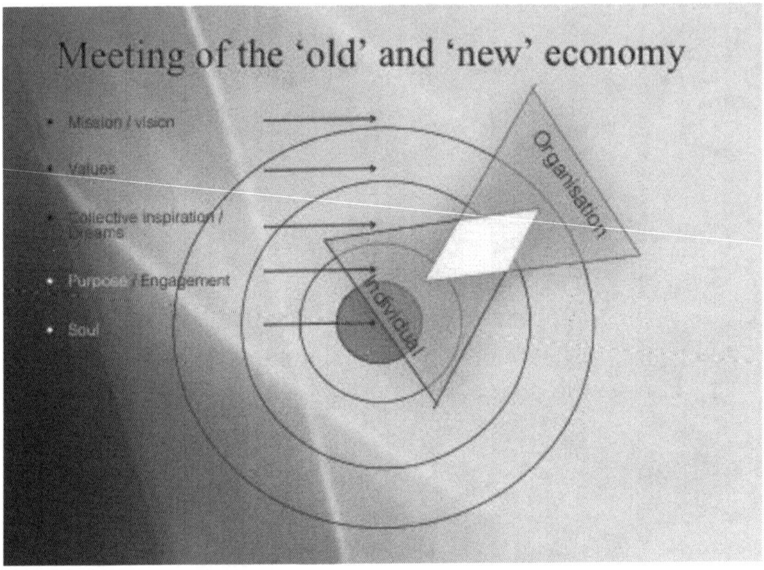


After collective inspiration – moving inwards – we focus more and more on the person, the individual. This is why coaches should be very alert to the topic of inspiration and really inquiring, together with the client and the community that surrounds them, into what we understand as inspiration, and how we can feed it and cultivate it. The managers and leaders that inspire will find themselves surrounded by people who often support the same values, the same mission and the same vision. For the coach it will of great importance to check with the client to what extent they are really leading by example, given that, as in the case of trust, we know that inspiration usually arrives on foot and leaves on horseback.

As Miriam Subirana says in her book *Appreciative Inquiry,* "Inspiring leaders bring out the best in people, they involve them in creating the vision and values of the organisation, in laying down the goals and objectives, and in designing the work process."

"Inspiring leaders balance the needs and interests of the employees, the clients and the business," states Cooperrider, "they strengthen excellence in others, as well as seeking it in themselves. They lead by example and show integrity in everything they do."[50]

The appreciative leader is an inspiring leader who communicates by motivating and inspiring. Let's therefore look at the second essential area: communication.

## Communication

The process of coaching or being coached begins with the understanding of the importance of communication. Open communication, even about the subjects that are considered to be challenges for the manager or leader. Some examples of the challenges I have faced myself were around concepts of power and hierarchy, trust and other values that differ from one culture to the next. In my time as a general manager, I learned that a considerable time was needed to construct a relationship that might be characterised by a high level of, at least, professional trust, which is absolutely necessary when we are striving to achieve open communication.

This immediately brings us face to face with one of the greatest challenges that managers and leaders have in communication, which is defined in questions such as: How much should I share? To what extent can I be transparent? Or: To what extent should I respect a local culture? These questions not only affect the specific organisation, but also the community in general where we carry out our activities.

In an appreciative inquiry coaching process where the community and staff also participate, this also supposes that we should have access to that community. Sometimes it can be done through conversations with people from the organisation; on occasion, sources such as cultural reports or an evaluation of, for example, Great Place to Work[51] are of great use. The problem tends to be that, often, the culture at hand can present a challenge when it comes to talking to all those we wish to involve: the teams, the staff of the organisation, and, if possible, including suppliers, clients and other interest groups.

I remember that in my time in a large organisation, where I was a member of one of the regional boards, we were asked the question: Do you maintain enough distance between yourselves (the board) and the employees? If you want open communication, you should get beyond that kind of question, and talk to the people that can contribute to the coaching process. One of the steps I took was to organise lunches once a month with about 6 employees, chosen at random from the organisation. At the beginning the people were guarded, but as the level of trust grew, those lunches turned into a fantastic tool to help open up the communication, and became a coaching instrument for me.

An open relationship between the coach and the client is fundamental in the coaching process. In this specific case, when the client is a manager or a leader, it is usually someone who spends most of their time exercising a position of power, and who has a good eye for hierarchies in organisations that often underline the levels of power. That position of power makes it even more difficult to maintain a high level of open communication and necessary trust to create the awareness that also includes experience, wisdom, integrity and even spirituality. It requires the courage to be vulnerable, and will lead to transparency.

I remember a golden rule that was given to me by one of the leaders I knew in my time at Apple Inc., who said: "Always try to bear in mind that transparent communication is everything." And of course there are things that, without a doubt, need to be dealt with confidentiality. But too often, we hold back information, for example, related to budgets, profit and loss accounts, market research, etc., for no more apparent reason than 'let's not share it, people won't understand it', 'they are not interested in it' or 'imagine what would happen if the outside world knew'.

If you want to coach a manager or leader so that they become the person in the organisation that people want to follow and who they trust, you should hold deep conversations with them on the importance of transparent communication. In the process of appreciative inquiry coaching, questions like, 'What do you think will happen if you share more or communicate about...' will be very useful in taking your client to another level of knowledge about communication. It will be important to hold the conversation with the manager or leader from the perspective of future that I have mentioned previously. The basic question would be: Can you see what it will bring you when you apply appreciative leadership? And, what, for you, is the incentive for evolving until you become an appreciative leader?

From my personal experience as a former executive, I have learned a great deal from the people who asked me questions about the meaning of the result of studies, like, for example, that of Great Place to Work. Open questions, aimed at giving meaning and therefore sharing, are great ways to coach someone on the road to becoming an appreciative leader.

As I commented at the start of this section, in order to have open communication, we need trust. Let us now look at this third essential area.

## Trust

Trust constitutes the solid basis of all positive and transparent communication: communication that involves and empowers people. Could the same be said for coaching in general, and appreciative inquiry coaching in particular? If we want a community to support someone, our client, so that they grow and evolve, then we should make sure that there is a solid base of trust, and this affects all the parties involved: the coach, the client and the interested community.

In the case of supporting someone to become an appreciative leader, there exists an aspect in relation to trust which is particularly important; it is the aspect of being capable of seeing the client's potential and their ambition to really devote themselves to developing and making this potential flourish. As Miriam explains in the introduction to this book, it is about seeing the oak in the acorn and making it grow.

The focal point of our coaching to help someone become the appreciative leader they want to be should be focused on the possibility and the ability to be cognisant of the potential they possess. This is a complex and stimulating journey, which is definitely valid for any process of coaching in which we might try to work with people who have the ambition not only to learn a particular skill, but who also really want to discover and understand themselves. To discover and understand who they really are and use it to serve an organisation, a community or even the world that they live in and that we share. All this begins with the basis of trust, trust in the competences and in the potential that one has, and that others need to see as well, or, at least, be aware of.

A well-known artist said once that the human beings that have been successful have understood the importance of trust as a basis, discipline as a practice, and concentration as an art, to achieve success. If we want to be successful as coaches and then, in particular, as coaches of those who aspire to become appreciative leaders, we should understand that these three elements are also valid for us. Bear in mind that both of you, coach and client, can have the need to be clear with regards to what kind of trust you are referring to when you speak of trust as the basis of your coaching process.

In our practice we often refer to the concept of professional trust, the trust that you have in the capacity of your client to become the appreciative leader that we have described previously in this chapter on sharing the definitions of Cooperrider and Whitney, Trosten-Bloom and Rader. This distinction is important, because there are very fine lines between the various kinds of trust that we know.

Sometimes appreciative leaders are defined as 'good parents', and this can generate confusion about the kind or level of trust that we are really talking about. The comparison around trust is then made from the perspective that it is about the potential and the ability to realise that potential from a professional perspective. Hence the use of 'professional trust', which is distinctly different from the 'unconditional trust' or love parents normally have for their children. There is a fine line here, which should be carefully observed when coaching from an appreciative perspective, or when coaching someone who aspires to grow as an appreciative leader. The borders are sometimes blurred and the challenge of fully trusting, receiving and embracing the potential of the other, and, at the same time, keeping a professional distance, becomes a serious challenge.

When we speak of trust, it should be clear that we are referring to the complexity of trusting oneself, and being trusted by others; they go hand in hand.

There are many kinds of trust. Let us look at some. The original one, with which we are born, is that of the baby that trusts its mother. Perhaps it is the deepest form of trust, given that it is unconditional. The mother feels trust from the moment the baby starts to grow inside her. When it is born, an unconditional trust arises between both of them.

Then we find trust between friends, who we connect with on an intellectual and emotional level; we rely on each other and we take care of each other.

In coaching for leaders, we talk about professional trust, in which we trust in the talents and competences of the other, and other bonds may not be made. This kind of trust exercises a great influence on the relationship of the leader with their team, and on the relationship between the coach and the client.

Key questions which both of them, the coach and the client, can come up against in this terrain of trust would be: How do I acquire trust as a leader in myself and in my behaviour? If I make mistakes that make me lose trust in myself, how do I get it back? How will the coach help me? Other impacting questions for reflection are: If I lose trust in my partners, colleagues and companions, how can I get it back? Or, if they lose trust in me, what can I do for them to get it back?

The fundamental question in this sense continues to be: Are you doing what this life is calling you to do, and do you trust your own answers after having taken some time to meditate upon it? On one occasion, David Cooperrider asked the essential question: Are you looking for your essence? Are you seeking your positive core?

In the process of asking these questions, and inquiring into their answers and the worlds that open up on talking about these subjects, it is necessary to be open to feedback. Let's look at this fourth essential area.

## Openness to feedback

In general we can say that (appreciative inquiry) coaching cannot exist without feedback and this, of course, is also valid when it comes to coaching someone on the road to becoming an appreciative leader. One of the assumptions in relation to feedback is that we should be able to build on what was written before about inspiration, communication and, above all, trust.

Another important element is the balance of power. One of the keys to being open to feedback lies in the belief that the people of an organisation, of a community, have a balance of power. This is usually an important factor with regards to trust. Only when there is a sense of a balanced situation, that there is a balance of power between the parties involved in the process, will we see that there can be a situation that allows for openness. Balanced meaning that there is no abuse of power, and therefore people feel secure in giving their feedback. It is important there is clarity in organisations with regards to ownership, authority and in relation to the decision-making power. The ideal situation is that in which someone listens to others with respect, and people know and believe that their feedback is taken into account.

Almost always in situations in which we deal with managers and leaders, we find ourselves in a dynamic in which, perhaps even subconsciously, one person has a certain kind of power over the other, and that includes us as coaches and clients. This kind of imbalance always influences the frankness of the conversation and feedback, although in a very subtle way, given that often we aren't aware of the unbalanced situation.

Other important factors that will have an influence on the frankness of the feedback is the attitude of the parties involved in the appreciative inquiry coaching process. An attitude that implies putting into practice humility, courage, appreciation and reflection. In general, demonstrating these attitudes will have a positive effect on each conversation. And in appreciative inquiry coaching, they are practised as principles. It is especially important when coaching someone on his path towards becoming an appreciative leader to pay attention to practices such as humility, courage, appreciation and reflection.[52] In the following I will look briefly at each one of these practices in relation to being open to feedback.

Given their positions, it tends to be something of a challenge for leaders to adopt a position of **humility**, since they are often expected to show strength in order to manage through power. However, in present-day society, the strength of the leaders, above all of an appreciative leader, resides in their ability to serve rather than dominate by force. It is a question of being a leader who understands how to serve. In today's society that means that, from the point of view of humility, they can continue to be highly respected leaders, but at the same time they will recognise that they don't know, they don't know everything. They will serve the people they have been entrusted with, and be aware that knowledge, and the wisdom of knowing, exist in the collective. If this is accepted, it constitutes one of the key elements for the success of people's openness to feedback. See more on the leader who serves in Subirana and Cooperrider (2013).[53]

It also requires **courage** from the leader's point of view to be open to the feedback they receive, not only from the coach but also in the appreciative inquiry coaching of the community. Simply because the feedback from the community will oscillate between approval and disapproval. Above all in the case of the less flattering feedback, one needs courage to fully accept that feedback as also being valuable and that it is given as a gift. Coaching a manager or leader so that they become an appreciative leader will require the coach to highlight the importance of this element, the bravery to open oneself to receiving feedback.

Which takes us to the third practice, that of **appreciation**. It is not only a question of the leader being open to feedback, but also that in fact the process of appreciative inquiry coaching goes one step further, in order to really appreciate and fully accept what is given as feedback, and together with the coach to try to understand the meaning of the feedback received. Frequently, it is much simpler to accept certain parts of the feedback, leaving aside others that are not considered important. The practice of appreciation tells us that we should accept all parts of the feedback, and try to understand them. But this practice doesn't mean that we have to like each bit of feedback that we are given!

Finally is the practice of **reflection**, which is one of the key elements for assessing feedback in an open way. It means that the coach and their client can sit down and think about questions such as: What have I learned or what can I learn from this feedback; or, what is the true gift that I have been given through this feedback? This practice will open up the way to accepting almost any kind of feedback, smoothing out the obstacles that can arise from the differences in power. In fact, this is valid for the four practices, and therefore it doesn't matter whether you are the coach or the client; they are important to both.

Having said this, it is very likely that it is a greater challenge for the (appreciative) leader to adopt these practices, given that they can be quite new and unfamiliar to us. And, when we say we, it is mainly the leader who should pay attention to that feedback. But, as I have already shown, the coach and the client will have to establish a relationship in which (professional) trust is key, and this means that the coach should also be receptive to the feedback that they might get from the client. A basic question with regards to this could be: Can you tell me your understanding of what I did, regarding the situation we are talking about? With regards to the feedback received by the coach, a possible question could be: How do you perceive my role in this coaching process?

In all this process, it is necessary to sustain a live and dynamic connection. Let us see the fifth essential area.

## Connection

Coaching for leaders revolves around the capacity to connect with all that there is. Naturally, this begins with the question of how the coach and the client connect. This is determined to a large extent by the factors we have described previously, such as the ability to establish an open and trusting relationship. However, in the case of appreciative inquiry coaching for leaders, with the specific objective of becoming an appreciative leader, the connection with all the other elements, and all the other members of the community, is also important. And, whilst it might seem easy to write about this area of connection, real life will present us with some challenges.

When we lead and motivate a large group, it is natural for us to feel different in relation to the diverse elements that are present, and to the people of that community; as a result there will also be a different level of connection to the diverse contributions, and the feedback that we might receive from the group. Nevertheless, it is of the greatest importance to stay connected to the community involved in the appreciative inquiry coaching process. It will have to be accepted that this connection will vary with the different members of the community, which is normal. The coach has an important role in this process, which consists of making sure that the client is aware of the importance of those connections, and also of their different consideration of the diverse feedbacks depending on where they come from (whether they come from someone external or internal, what the power is in the relationship, their place in the hierarchy…). The success of the coaching process and the journey to becoming an appreciative leader depends on maintaining open, positive relationships and positive connections with the community in general. See more on this aspect on dealing with the principle of wholeness on page 97, and on social constructionism on page 64.

Maintaining good connections with all involved parties requires a balance that we need to find. Let's look at the sixth essential area.

## In search of balance

Much of what I have put forward in this chapter can be summed up in a certain way in the title of this section. The constant search for the right balance in what we do is key to any process, including the coaching ones. What can be added is the element of balance from the performance perspective, and through the prism of appreciative inquiry coaching. The traditional ways of coaching managers and leaders usually focus on the terrain of performance, and of endeavour. In traditional coaching for leaders, the focus resides in the data, the objectives, the control and the action related to this. Sometimes 360º feedback is used, but almost always to reveal 'one single truth', the truth of the shareholders' value. It is there that keeping balance in the appreciative inquiry coaching of leaders comes in, and, in particular, when it is a question of coaching managers and leaders to become appreciative leaders. This only occurs if the clients understand that they should keep the balance between, on the one hand, information, the data and knowledge, and, on the other, the experience, wisdom, integrity and even spirituality that we can find in organisations and in our workplaces in general. Only when the coach, the community that plays a role in the appreciative inquiry coaching, and the client understand the importance of this balance will we be able to see the evolution of managers and leaders towards the appreciative leaders of the future.

Naturally, the challenge is that finding that balance, as the words themselves indicate, is a dynamic process. So there is no status quo, but only an evolving and changing situation that requires all those involved to reflect on what that balance might be in the moment, and what should be done to maintain that balance. As can be easily understood, this dynamic nature is one of the aspects that presents a great challenge for appreciative inquiry coaching in general, and more specifically, for training leaders to become appreciative leaders. In the coaching process we can ask: Try to describe a situation that you consider to be balanced enough to progress – as a certain unbalance is also needed to create movement. What is needed for the balance not to get stuck or too comfortable, but rather for it to maintain it dynamic enough for all those in the organisation, including you, to be alert and active? And, how do you see the response of the people who work with you to, for example, the technological developments? How do you feel that their talents, skills and competences respond to the new situations that arise?

Pay attention to the practices mentioned above (humility, courage, appreciation and reflection); practising them will be key to maintaining that balance, whereby an additional challenge will be the complexity of the system involved in the coaching process. It is a complex system of coach, client and community, all of which have an important contribution to make to the whole process of appreciative inquiry coaching and coaching a manager or leader to grow an understanding of appreciative leadership and possibly becoming an appreciative leader.

To end this chapter I want to emphasise a last essential aspect for the success of the coaching; it concerns commitment in the relationship. Let us look at it.

## Commitment in the coaching relationship

In my beginnings with coaching, in the 80s at Apple Inc., we used to work from the same perspective that we were earning our living from – the transactional perspective. We all know it: you obtain something and, in exchange, you pay for it. A transaction takes place, and this is something deeply rooted in societies all over the world. Once the transaction ends, very often the relationship also ends. That is, the transaction ends in all aspects. In today's society, we often hear complaints about follow-up service.

In the world of training, consulting and coaching, things usually work in the same way. After an hour of coaching, the client is charged, and once the bill is paid, it is over.

In the world of appreciative inquiry coaching, things are different. Yes, of course there continues to be a transactional element in the coaching process, but as the coaching process in itself has become what we call these days a transformative process, we should commit ourselves in another way, and it is here that commitment comes in. The most striking aspect in this sense is that appreciative inquiry coaching consists of connectivity, a true connection between all the parties involved in the coaching process. And this is valid for all those who train or are trained in an appreciative way.

Appreciative inquiry has to do with connecting to our positive core. This is what makes this kind of coaching for leaders so special; it is why there is a growing interest amongst leaders to understand why we do the things we do, and this goes further than obtaining more profits. It has to do with the ambition of doing good for the world, not just for the shareholders. This requires, as has been said, a deep commitment from all the involved parties: the coach, the community and the client. We usually begin by asking the following questions of each of them: How much do you fully commit yourself to participating in this process, and, to what point does your commitment go; how much are you prepared to give up?

The transformative journey is a journey that raises numerous challenges. It involves all the elements described in this chapter and the awareness that it often isn't easy to attain them. But, if we take them seriously, if we are committed to them, committed to each other, and perhaps above all committed to ourselves, to our own journey towards our positive essence – there are those who refer to our spiritual being, our soul – we will have many possibilities of helping each other to evolve and grow as individuals.

Growing as individuals and increasing our collective wisdom by coaching others – and above all, the leaders of our world – will undoubtedly create a world in which it will be worth living. However, we will have to go beyond the transaction to reach the world in which we will find an unconditional commitment to coach each other appreciatively. If we all, coaches, clients and their communities, embrace that idea, we might be able to show those who occupy positions of leadership the broad perspective necessary to make of our world a vibrant and beautiful place with room for everybody.

# 19. Ethical code of appreciative inquiry coaching

The ICF, International Coaching Federation, has created an ethical code for the coaching profession which can be found on their website (www.coachfederation.org). We could add other elements to this code that would constitute the code of ethical practice of appreciative inquiry coaching. They would cover the following subjects:

### *As coach*

Commitment and effort to live appreciatively.

Living the appreciative in order to prepare oneself before the sessions.

Incorporating appreciation into your way of life.

Living the principles of appreciative inquiry.

Commitment and self-care in order to be well.

Training oneself in humility.

Being convinced that all stories have positive aspects, thus enabling us to integrate the past by embracing it. In turn, this permits us to see positive images of the future.

### *Relationship with the client*

Space of relational horizontality.

Installing values in the relationship.

Non-instructive character.

Accompanying the other as thinking partner.

Appreciative acceptance.

Not judging.

Invoking the positive.

Reinforcing the positive.

Promoting appreciation.

Respecting the client's pace.

Facilitating autonomy.
Respecting the spaces of the client and sustaining their field.

### *Coaching style*

Inclusion of the client's relational system as part of the coaching.
Define, Discover, Dream, Design and Destiny in the process of the sessions.
Working with the positive core.
Being appreciative in our feedback.
Appreciative questions.
Recognising the client's competences.

# Part IV

# The person who accompanies another/others. The accompanier. The coach.

Embodied in transitory organic structures, human life is characterised by the exclusive capacity to think, imagine, go into the infinite space of the spirits. It is from here that the presence is projected, from the inner power, of which it is necessary to be fully aware for its opportune usage. And for trust in oneself, a vital condition for the presence to be 'effective' in the personal dimensions (internal) and the collective (external, relational). The ideal is to obtain the benefits of the 'reciprocal presence' (in oneself and in others).

It is necessary to share. Share with others. Be compassionate. Be crazy about something. It is necessary to not let oneself get trapped by routine, by pessimism. Creative excess is our hope. The future, I like repeating this, is still to be made.

The world must change. Another world is possible, but we must, in the first instance, change ourselves.
– Federico Mayor Zaragoza[54]

# 20. The coach

An appreciative inquiry coach is a practitioner and expert in appreciative inquiry. The tools they use for their practice are directed at valuing and developing the best of the person. They ask them questions formulated according to appreciative inquiry which foster a connection to their positive core, that is, to the seed of their personal power and 'the sap' that maintains their vitality. They ask questions to strengthen and encourage the discovery and recognition of the talent and capacities of the person they are accompanying, their client, to enable them to manifest and serve the dream they wish to live. The coach offers people the possibility of discovering their own capacities and of making them flourish.

The appreciative coach consistently demonstrates the principles of appreciative inquiry in all their interactions. They live and apply the ten principles of appreciative inquiry in their life and their professional practice. They live them and express them through their presence, their words and the questions that they ask themselves and others. I explored the principles in chapter 14.

An appreciative coach lives more in the questions than in the answers. They don't feel that they have to give answers and are comfortable in the zone of 'not knowing', the 'I don't know'. They trust in their client's capacity for learning and encourage it. They always work towards not being needed, not being indispensable.

They are someone who listens, appreciating value and recognising what gives energy and vitality to the person telling their story. They collaborate in bringing out the potential and skills of the person they coach. They encourage the appreciative point of view, allowing people to find the available resources that are invisible to 'the untrained eye'. That way they nurture the positive emotions that motivate people to continue with the process.

Other features that characterise the appreciative inquiry coach are:

- They accompany the client in defining the topics of the sessions affirmatively, using a positive language that describes what they want and distances them from what they don't want, and from the language of deficit typical of problem solving.
- They motivate the client to find innovations and strategies.
- They ask questions that allow people to identify their inner dialogues, so that they can observe the quality of the same.
- They make it possible for the client to find their guiding images.

The living and practice of all this causes a cognitive, emotional, perceptive and behavioural opening, which improves performance, and helps to consider possibilities for the future and change. On a bodily level, the parasympathetic nervous system is activated, which produces well-being and health. Boyatzis reminds us that "taking into account that a coaching relationship is a form of power relationship, like leadership, in which a person is open to being influenced by another, the states of mind, ideas and even the habits of the coach can be extended to the client and vice versa."[55]

In the face of the person's unhappiness, suffering or pain, the appreciative inquiry coach doesn't attempt to relieve their pain, but rather maintains the intention of focusing on helping them in their development and growth. So, they accompany them on a journey which goes from the past and present pain to perceiving the attractor images of the future they want to live. And, on seeing them, on living through them in the visualisation and narrating them, the client leaves the space of the pain, motivated to go towards where they want to go. They connect to what gives them light and life.

# 21. Thinking partner

The appreciative inquiry coach can also be a thinking partner. A thinking partner holds the space of the client. Beyond their words, the person generates a field, and the thinking partner sustains it for them. A thinking partner is an appreciative inquiry coach who not only takes the client's individual aspirations and talents into account (as in traditional coaching); they also take the context into account: who they work with (aligning personal strengths and values with the system of the organisation; the impact of the person on the system they work and live together in). The thinking partner keeps in mind that the person develops in the context of their system. Therefore, it is not only a matter of defining and achieving their personal objectives in their own terms, but rather of including the whole system in the vision, in the conversation and the actions. The coach becomes a thinking partner of the client.

The thinking partner accompanies the client in passing through different stages in a process of individual sessions. Firstly, they identify the areas they want to work in, and define two or three affirmative topics that will act as a framework for the accompaniment. The thinking partner asks some questions in order for the client to discover highlights of their life in which they experienced events related to the chosen topics. In the questions, we include the environment of the clients, their relationships, their impact on that environment and its impact on them, how they gave life to the positive core, how they contributed and what elements of their environment made it easier for the core to prosper.

In sum, the thinking partner accompanies the client in thinking about their priorities and those of their family, their organisation, their team, the area they work in, and the community they are immersed in. They awaken an appreciative perspective which includes their environment, and values how their positive core contributes to the development of all the stakeholders (collaborators, clients, students, volunteers, workers, relationships in their team, suppliers, business partners, family, friends, etc.). They also reflect on how their environment contributes to nourishing their personal positive core.

In the *Design* phase, the thinking partner asks the client questions to guide them in formulating their proposals of possibilities and provocative declarations. They accompany them in reflecting on what conversations are pending, with requests, offers and commitments which will help to put the formulated proposals and declarations into practice. In this way, the thinking partner accompanies people through questions and reflections so that they can go through a complete process of appreciative inquiry on an individual level.

The thinking partner doesn't always ask questions; in this they differ from the coach. Rather, they generate an appreciative space in which the accompanied person feels comfortable. If the person is sad, for example, the thinking partner holds the sadness in the relational field generated between them; they don't ask, but simply hold the sadness in the field, they don't go into looking at it in more depth or talking about it, they just hold it, feel it, recognise it and, in so doing, the sadness is diluted. In the community of appreciative coaches and thinking partners, we find quite a lot of people who practise Buddhism. We can establish various connections between both practices. One of them is the practice of sustaining the so-called negative emotions, anger, fear, sadness, not inquiring into them, but not escaping from them; on holding them, they dissolve and the connection to the positive core, the essence, the inner light reappears.

One of the keys to holding the space in the relationship with the person we are accompanying is the power of an appreciative and transformative presence. Let's consider it now.

# 22. Presence[56]

The power of presence is the power to be yourself and have an impact around you just by being present. When you are present, you are alert and attentive, and you are aware. You observe, and you see the visible and feel the invisible. You are connected. Connected to yourself, to the other and to the universe. You feel whole, and from wholeness your being overflows with positive energy. Wherever you go, at each step, you emanate trust, happiness and hope.

The power of presence arises from a clear intention and an open attitude. The intention of the appreciative inquiry coach includes that of generating trust, openness and appreciation, leading the client to connect to their positive core and live the appreciative principles that we saw in chapter 14.

As a coach I try to live my presence by integrating body and emotion, mind and spirit, intuition and reason. Most of us have been brought up to function on a daily basis from the neck up. We learn to trust more in our mind than in our body when it comes to acting in the world. In not integrating mind and body, we lose valuable information that we might otherwise obtain from being more aware of all of our being. When you are in someone's physical presence, what does your body tell you? Listen to it, and you will be more present and aware of what is happening as it happens.

It is a question of realising the importance of non-verbal language. When all your energies are aligned, that is, your awareness, your decision, your thoughts, what you feel, do and express, there isn't a contradiction between what you want to say, what you say and what you feel. Sometimes, there are people who say one thing with their mouth, but their body gives off another message. The person isn't aligned. The body doesn't lie. Bodily, you transmit what your soul feels. Despite the attempt to hide it with a well-prepared speech, the body doesn't lie. If you give out a contradictory message – one message with words and a different one with the body – your presence is diminished and you confuse the other, or cause them to reject you. It is about knowing that, for your words to be influential, you should be connected to what you transmit, to the message you give. It is about believing what you say and feeling what you say.

Before beginning a coaching session, I focus on being fully present, open and connected. Present in mind and body. I breathe deeply, I observe that my body position is open and welcoming, and that my body is sitting straight, in a dignified and alert position. As Eckhart Tolle says: "When you listen to another person, don't only listen with your mind, listen with all your body." What is your posture like when your body is predisposed to listen, and to feel what it listens to?

Let us touch on the factors that contribute to increasing our power of presence. This will help us to understand why some speakers, lecturers, coaches and leaders have more presence than others. Why, in some meetings, one person has more presence than another, who goes almost unnoticed. Why some people become visible, and others remain invisible.

A person with presence is anchored within and firm. They achieve that firmness from being centred in their positive core: in the sap feeding it from the inside. They are rooted in the present moment like a tree. Their presence comes from having and feeling an appreciative attitude. It is a presence that recognises and is recognised. It is a transformative presence.

They are anchored in their values, and in their experience, in their inner wisdom and emotional maturity. They are their roots. The roots nourish the trunk of their self-esteem and give them the firmness of being present. They don't need to pretend or prove anything. They are present. Their branches are their different expressions of being, through work, their profession, their relationships and actions.

The deepest reason for the lack of peace and the abundance of anger, fear and mistrust, be it in personal experience or in human relationships, lies in the loss of awareness of our authentic identity and true nature of being. We tend to base our identity on the physical aspect (body), actions (what we do/the roles we play), possessions (what we accumulate), place (where we come from physically), and our conditioning (acquired beliefs). Basing your self-esteem on any of these aspects can become a problem, because none of them is permanent. If you accompany someone, and are centred in your authentic identity, you will be able to take on the person's restlessness and unhappiness, helping them to transcend it. With your centred presence, you act as a mirror. You don't need to do anything else, nor say anything special. Being present, you generate a vibrational field that accompanies the other in reaching more authentic aspects of their identity.

In appreciative coaching, we inquire to discover the positive core and connect to it. When energy flows from the roots to the leaves, the presence is felt in each moment and each expression of that person. Let's remember that the positive core is made up of the essential values, of what gives meaning to life, optimum experiences, strengths, qualities, what revitalizes, is life-giving and energises the person, making them shine in their full potential.

To be like that tree, healthy, strong and present, you need to pay attention to keeping your inner channels open. Without blockages, without saboteurs, without fears that interfere and limit that flow of energy. Be connected to your essence. Don't get lost in creating an image and trying to be what you aren't.

Your presence increases on freeing yourself of the world's mirages and conditionings. You dissolve the tensions. You allow yourself to be transparent without pretending. You don't make judgements and you accept. You accept because you have taken social constructionism on board, allowing you to embrace multiple perspectives. Out of acceptance, you embrace the moment and people as they are and feel. Even though you don't agree, acceptance helps you to not resist what it is. That way your presence is transformative. You transform out of acceptance and love. Out of resistance, violence or irritation, you confront but you do not transform.

To do this, you only have to connect to your roots: to your essence. You live the values that move you, and give meaning to your existence. You uphold the beliefs that allow you to be and flow. You question and leave to one side those beliefs that limit you and prevent you from shining. You shine when you feel whole.

Another aspect to bear in mind in order for our presence to be transformative is related to the intention. Review your intentions and motivations. Why are you going to say what you are going to say? Why are you going to do what you are going to do? What moves you? Does what you will say or do take the other into account? Are you on the path that is good for you, or are you going to go off-track, weaken and get stuck? Will it free you and will it free the other? Is it what is best for everybody? Remember that the actions that benefit you also benefit others. The actions that are not good for us are also not good for others. "The moment you realise how important it is to love yourself, you will stop making others suffer."[57] With full awareness, you can break the chains that keep you trapped in the never-ending circle of desire and rejection. You recognise the desire without getting trapped by it.

When you sustain your aim in your consciousness, the power of the intention acts with force: you create what you believe in. Desires and intentions can change the physical manifestation of reality. In the silence, connect to your aim and intention so that a deeper meaning impregnates what you do.

Your actions have influence. Your presence goes together with your actions. If you lose connection to your centre, your essence, your action is emptied of meaning. It is routine. You act out of obligation and responsibility, not excitement. Your action does not have the light of a heartfelt presence. Before the coaching session, feel that you are going to accompany the person from your loving presence; that you are going to listen and feel out of a full presence.

The power of the appreciative attitude manifests itself even in silence. It is an attitude that is active, positive, aware and trusting. Let us briefly describe them:

### *An active attitude*

You are actively present. Your listening is active, that is, your mind doesn't go off-track. You are responsible for your answers, that is, for what you ask.

### *A positive attitude*

You have a broad vision and perception of your internal and external reality, and you focus on what strengthens you and strengthens others. You contribute to the person with you focusing on what strengthens both them and the members of their relational network.

### *An aware attitude*

This is about being completely awake and alert. Aware that you are the creator of your thoughts and feelings. Not a victim but rather someone who has mastery over their being.

### *An attitude of trust*

Trust in the people you have before you: I place my trust in you. When you trust in yourself, you dare to be creative and respond with ease to situations, people and events. When you trust, you are open to dialogue, support and mutual learning, to the creative initiative. You are a source of inspiration which, with your presence, allows others to let go and be creative. Your trust allows the uncovering and flourishing of your resources, and those of your client.

For your presence to be transformative it is necessary to know what it is that weakens you. Up till here we have seen what strengthens us. Now let's look at what weakens us, and how to counteract it.

## What diminishes your presence?

### *Mental confusion*

When you do something without being sure that you want to do it, doubting whether you should, being afraid of failing and doubting as to whether you will achieve it, whatever it is that you do, with that doubt, you won't have the strength of clarity. However, when you do something based on your values, a clear vision, a state of self-esteem, of trust, of serenity and well-being, with clarity, concentration and centred, you will be more successful, you will be more assertive and you will have the ability to see it through.

### *Not being present in body, heart and mind*

You are misaligned. Your mind goes in one direction. Your heart feels differently. Your body is rigid. You don't flow in the present. You are somewhere else. You have left your core. Meditating makes you present. See chapter 23 on meditation and mindful coaching.

### *Negative thoughts*

When your thoughts are negative, you don't value what you are or what you have. Your presence is in a reality created by your mind, not in reality. Your mind dominates you. You don't appreciate. You aren't present. Your thoughts aren't constructive. Sometimes you think a lot. On thinking too much, you disconnect from your essential being; you get entangled in the web of your useless thoughts. Your thoughts lose authenticity, direction and meaning. You complain. You see what is going wrong. Your conversation goes into a spiral of destructive or useless criticism.

Connect to what inspires you. Open yourself to beauty. Remember a highlight of your life. Evoke a positive image.

## *Guilt*

We feel guilty when we don't do what we have set out to do, when we transgress a rule that we have internalised as one we must live by, when our reaction is out of place. Pushed by a longing for freedom, transgression or curiosity, we cross the limits we had marked out for ourselves. On crossing those limits, a feeling of guilt arises. A voice points out to us that we shouldn't have done it.

Guilt is moral self-reproach: I did something wrong when I could have done it differently. An act of integrity can set to rights the guilt that arises through harming integrity. The difficulty arises when the guilt makes us feel unworthy, because then it doesn't allow for correction; it only leaves room for punishment. That is a state without full awareness that leaves us trapped in guilt.

When a critical thought brings on a feeling of guilt, it generates self-punishment. You feel bad, and on top of that, you punish yourself, getting trapped in a spiral of guilt and punishment that can lead to a situation taking on tragic dimensions.[58]

On accompanying someone who feels guilty we can inquire into: How to set the situation to rights by carrying out an act of integrity. What acts would be whole in that situation? What pact or belief has been transgressed? Do you want to continue to uphold that pact? If the answer is yes, then saying sorry can put the situation right. If the answer is no, then another field of inquiry opens up, to do with the beliefs that are no longer valid for him or her.

### *Inner critic*

When we decide that we are going to incorporate a practice, transform a habit or strive towards an objective, what usually happens is that a self-boycott intervenes. We boycott our own aims. Discipline helps us to overcome our saboteur and the inner critic which places obstacles in front of our intentions. It is doubts and fears that hold us back and block us. The inner critic makes us give up when we want to be creative and we have ideas that go beyond our routine and what we already know.

On accompanying someone in the coaching sessions we have to pay attention to silencing our inner critic. Only then will our presence be appreciative and transformative.

### *Being absent. Where are you?*

Your body is here, but your heart is somewhere else. Your mind wanders. You are here but you are not present. For example, when the client says something to you that triggers a memory, a worry about a similar situation and concern of your own, without realising, your mind starts thinking about your own preoccupation, and during those moments, you stop being present for the other. 'You have gone'. For this not to happen, it helps to learn mental control and mindfulness. Meditation is a good practice for achieving this. I speak to you about it in the next section.

### *Mental distractions*

We generate some fifty thousand thoughts a day. Many are unnecessary. There are thoughts that are poetry and an expression of beauty; they are inspiring and they lift you. Other thoughts are like storms that lash at you. Unnecessary thoughts are thoughts that come up in inopportune moments. They are thoughts of worry and disquiet that appear in the mind. They don't have any constructive use; they are not generative; neither are they particularly negative.

Unnecessary and useless thoughts might be referring to the past: "If only that hadn't happened." "Why did they have to say that to me?" Too many thoughts about something that we can't change now. They are also about the future: what is going to happen tomorrow, how is it going to happen? "What will I do if I end up alone?" They are quick, repetitive, useless thoughts, and they get you nowhere. They weaken your ability to concentrate. You get distracted. If you have a lot of such thoughts, you use more energy and time to carry out each task. What is more, they cause negativity, irritation and impatience.

When the client expresses themselves out of mental distraction, it is important not to follow them in their story. Return to the centre, to the agreed subject. Don't let yourself get carried away out of the curiosity that the story might awaken in you, because then both of you will end up distracted, and far from the subject chosen to be inquired into.

### *Tension*

You are not comfortable. Something is upsetting you and causing you tension. On not being relaxed, your tense presence causes unease around you. Meditate before a session of accompaniment or coaching to relax yourself.

### *Worries*[59]

Each person has their worries: their health, their children, work, the traffic, the public debt, wars, the nuclear threat, climate change, etc. A method for checking to what extent you are a positive person consists of examining what you invest your thoughts, time and energy in. Some of the things that worry you are outside of your control; you can't change them, and we can call this an area of concern. There are other things that you can do something about, and this would be your area of influence.

An example of an area for concern: However much I worry and obsess about unemployment and how difficult it is to find work, that won't make it easier for me to find a good job.

Reactive people focus their efforts on the area for concern. Their attention is on other people's defects, the problems around them, and circumstances over which they lack control. From this come feelings of guilt, accusations, destructive criticisms, a reactive language and feelings of impotence. They want others to change first, or circumstances, and feel that they won't change until this is the case. The negative energy generated as a consequence of this approach, combined with the lack of attention towards the areas in which something *could* be done, reduces the area of possible influence.

When we enter our area of concern, we give those matters the power to control and dominate us. In so doing, we neither create nor strengthen the positive attitude necessary to effect positive change.

In the coaching session, make sure you work on the areas of influence. You can accompany the client in releasing the tension caused by focusing on areas of concern about which they can have no influence on making a real change.

### *Projections*

Instead of taking responsibility for how you feel, you project blame on to others and on to your environment. You create an illusory reality, surrounded by a reflection of your own projection, and you aren't aware of the different perspectives of reality. You only see yours under your prism and your projection. In projections you make judgements according to your point of view. You need to broaden your way of seeing, aware that your story is not the only one dictating reality, but that we all construct reality together. Living social constructionism as we have seen it opens us to accepting multiple perspectives (pages 64).

## *Comparing yourself* [60]

It is a human habit to make comparisons and compare ourselves with each other. When comparing yourself leads you to feel inferior or superior, you create prejudices and an erroneous idea of privilege. That is, comparing divides: it makes you feel inferior or superior, depending on whether you have more or less privilege. If you have less, you nurture the false belief that you are not worthy or good enough.

Pay attention to the situations in which you allow someone to impress you, and you compare yourselves with them. Being impressed isn't a bad thing, but you can fall into the tendency of staying trapped in the superfluous and in appearances. What impresses you, influences you, and even moulds your awareness in that moment. You lose the ability to create your thoughts and feelings, and these are influenced by the impression that you have allowed the other person to leave on you. Sometimes the impression is so great that you lose yourself in it. You give up your power to the other.

When you compare yourself to others without accepting your present, you want what the other has, their properties, their talents, their achievements. Instead of being grateful for what you have, and accepting yourself as you are, you try to have what they have and be like them. In this way, you are never satisfied. The dissatisfaction causes you a constant unhappiness and loss of vitality.

In the coaching sessions, or even in conversation with one or another friend, when you see that the other, whether client, friend or family, compares themselves in such a way as to feel weak and inferior, you can ask them to talk to you about someone who is a source of inspiration to them, and inquire into what it is that the other has that inspires them. Lead them to make a healthy comparison which motivates them to improve and transcend themselves.

### *Permanent dissatisfaction*

Our consumer society has created a culture of accumulation and materialism which, however much we have, does not satisfy us. It is a mirage that generates an apparent satisfaction inside us. But when you look in the mirror of your heart you find sadness, suffering and emptiness. Dissatisfaction. Erich Fromm already said it: "If you are not happy with everything you already have, you won't be happy either with everything that you don't have."

We live in uncertain times, often overwhelmed by insecurity. We have a lot, and everything is available. We can choose. Even so, dissatisfaction seems to be a constant. The sensation of lack causes a state of constant need. Emotional need hides the essential desire, the true need to fill an existential and spiritual void. On attempting to satisfy that emotional need through physical means, or sensorial experiences (purely genital sex – or not even that, in the case of Internet pornography – drink, drugs and other externalised and expansive forms that create dependencies in us), the emptiness is perpetuated, as well as harming us and damaging our health. Pursuing the satisfaction of superfluous desires, one remains in a lack of awareness: yet to discover their essential desire, their deepest dream, and life's ideal.

To overcome these debilitating challenges, I suggest being mindful, heartful and meditating. Let's see how.

# 23. Meditation and mindful coaching

*Sati*, in Pali, the original language of the Buddhist literature, Theravada, is usually translated into English as mindfulness, and Spanish as full attention. Mindfulness is concentration in the mind. It consists of impartial observation, one that perceives without taking sides. It is about the state of being stripped of favouritisms. It is the awareness of the present moment. It takes place here and now, in an attitude of alertness. It allows for the contemplation of phenomena without depending on the ideas associated with the I, the me, and mine. It consists of being aware of what you are thinking while you think it, of what happens while it happens.

With full attention, and mindfulness, you notice when you get distracted or stray from your aim. On noticing, you return to it easily. Thoughts turn into a fog, preventing us from seeing and feeling clearly. As these habits of thinking in an accelerated fashion, the mind occupied and reactive, get stronger, our heart empties and stays hungry for the fresh air of love. Through full awareness we get back the fresh air.

Attention is the necessary key to living free from limiting conditionings and being fully aware, able to own your life and your reactions; taking care of the other, your environment and yourself. Pay attention to what you think, be awake, alert and be an observer. In this way you will stay connected to the external layers of your identity (your body, your role, your position, and the things you have to do), at the same time as to your inner awareness (what you are and what your being longs for). You will be rooted in your awareness, observing from there what you think and do. It is the 'third eye' that sees and pays attention.

That is why I propose that perhaps instead of full attention we ought to speak of full awareness. The master Thich Nhat Hanh, when referring to *Sati*, speaks of full awareness. But teachers from other schools translate it as full attention and the ability to free oneself from stress. Full awareness helps us much more than simply relaxing us and helping us to overcome stress.

In fact, one of the extraordinary effects of the practice of meditation is that it stimulates our self-healing system. The power of belief and the image you associate with it helps you to improve your health. I am referring to the so-called placebo effect. The power of thought can cause a person to cure themselves or become ill, to lower or raise their temperature. As I developed in the book *Indagación Apreciativa* [*Appreciative Inquiry*] (2013) on the power of the image in our life, on evoking guiding images and believing in them, we are mobilising all our inner system, of emotional, bodily and mental health, and our external one in our interactions. In his work *The Human Options* (1981), Norman Cousins, faculty member of the school of medicine at UCLA (University of California, Los Angeles), suggests that, beyond the central nervous system, the hormonal system and the immune system, there are another two systems not conventionally taken into account, which, however, should be recognised as essential to the correct workings of the human being: the healing system and the belief system. Cousins (1983)[61] argues that the two work together: "The healing system is the way the body mobilises all its resources to combat disease. The belief system is often the activator of the healing system."

Joe Dispenza,[62] chiropractic doctor, biochemist and neuroscientist, decided not to be operated on after having a serious accident. He wanted to experience in himself the capacity for self-healing. He was risking remaining paralysed. Fascinated by the achievements, he began research in people who have had a remission of their illness, and were cured by an apparently 'magic' effect. He wanted to see what these people had in common. His discoveries are a revelation. The result of his research shows us the importance of the attention and meditation for changing our habits. He explains to us that if we don't manage to think beyond our emotions, we will live according to what the environment imposes on our body. Instead of thinking, innovating and believing, we will only activate the synaptic memories of other areas of the brain, based on our genetic inheritance, or our personal past; we will continue in the routine. We will be at the mercy of the effect instead of being the creators of the cause. Attention is the key to changing this automatic functioning.

Your attention allows you to direct energy towards whatever you want. However, you should be attentive and decide with great care where you want to direct your energy! Sometimes you fix your attention on to the future that causes you anxiety or you anchor it in the past that causes you anguish. Then, instead of being your ally, it entangles you. The past torments you, and the future causes you anxiety. Your attention keeps you blocked in. You should change the focus of your attention in order to get away from the torment or the anxiety.

Attention, will and concentration have to go hand in hand. Whatever it is that you give attention to in your life grows and lights up. If you focus on a problem, you increase it. If you focus on what works and on your strengths, you invoke them and express them. Full attention, whole attention, is to be alert, noticing and aware of what is happening in you, and around you.

Meditation implies silencing the mind, focusing, being present and managing the emotions and inner critic positively.

Meditation helps the coach to:

- Listen beyond the words.
- Not judge.
- Be fully present.
- Go beyond the rational mind.
- Connect to the intuition.
- Be an impartial observer.

- Broaden the field of infinite possibilities.
- Trust in yourself and in your resources.
- Do meditative practices.
- Be capable of visualising and making the other visualise, that is, of evoking guiding images.

Let's look at each one of these aspects:

### *Listen beyond the words*

Sometimes what the client says is not really what their soul wants to express. From a meditative state, the coach can read and understand between the words. Their listening is whole. Their 'third ear' is alert and working. Then, in the conversation, we move forward, not so much through listening by fixing on to the world of objects and facts, but by entering into listening to the story of an essential being that is alive and in evolution. Otto Scharmer[63] talks to us of generative listening: "I cannot express what I experience in words. My whole being has slowed down. I feel more quiet and present and more my real self. I am connected to something larger than myself. This form of listening moves beyond the current field, and connects us to an even deeper realm of emergence. I call this level of listening, generative listening, or listening from the emerging field of future possibility. This level of listening requires us to access not only our open heart, but also our open will, our capacity to connect to the highest future possibility that can emerge. We no longer look for something outside. […] in this listening process, you realize that by the end of the conversation you are no longer the same person you were when it began. You have gone through a subtle but profound change that has connected you to a deeper source of knowing, including the knowledge of your best future possibility and self."

## *Not judge*

It is important to create an atmosphere where 'nobody is wrong'. Not to judge is to allow the client to express themselves freely. Judgements are like obstacles on the path. As we have already seen, it is possible to not let the saboteur and the inner critic of the coach appear during the session. Accepting where the client is and not judging them will enable them to see an open road to travel, one without obstacles.

## *Be fully present*

Meditation focuses you, and as a coach it is important to be fully present. At the time of the session, the client should feel that he or she is the most important thing for you. It is good to meditate ten minutes before the session so that, when it begins, the client enters an atmosphere of presence and centredness.

Boyatzis shares with us that "the studies that use magnetic resonance in the brain throw light on the neuronal mechanisms of coaching. For the coach to help to greater effect, they could consider the role played by the negative and positive emotional attractors in the coach-client relationship, bearing in mind that there are destabilizing forces that create psycho-physiological states that can foster the process of change and others that can stall it."[64] We should work on our presence in order to generate positive states; that is why I devoted chapter 22 to this subject, and if you want to know more, I recommend the book I published in 2012, *El poder de nuestra presencia: una guía de coaching espiritual* [*The Power of Our Presence: A Guide to Spiritual Coaching*].

Meditation helps us so that our presence stimulates the positive emotional attractors, whose effect is to improve the well-being of the coach, the client and their mutual relationship.

## *Go beyond the rational mind*

With meditation the mental and rational 'chatter' ceases. You stop analysing, planning, rationalising. That way you leave room for the intuition. You listen better and are capable of maintaining the field as a thinking partner (chapter 21). It is easier for the right question to appear out of the intuition.

### *Connect to the intuition*

Intuition is key to knowing what question to ask, at what moment; to feel what is needed; to understand the client and to guide the session in the best way possible. With intuition, you can dance in the moment, accompanying the client in their process with harmony and complicity. With intuition, you connect to your innate wisdom, as I explained on page 18, opening up the channel for the other person to connect to their wisdom too.

### *Be an impartial observer*

Meditation turns the coach into an impartial observer. That way, the coach doesn't have an opinion, in the sense that they don't come down on one side or the other. They accept different ways of looking and perspectives. The coach observes the process of the client without 'getting into it'. They flow and accompany, they dance in the moment, but they don't 'get caught on' whatever it is that the client is going through. In this way, they are not influenced by either the negativity or the energy that the client projects on to them.

### *Broaden the field of infinite possibilities*

Meditating helps you to transcend limitations. You leave behind limiting beliefs, perceptions and judgements. .In the meditative state, the coach generates a magnet for the client to also get out of their limitations and broaden the field of infinite possibilities.

### *Trust in yourself and in your resources*

When you trust in yourself you awaken the other's trust in you more strongly. Beginning the session in a serene state allows you to keep your store of inner resources open. You realise that you can, and you have a lot to offer.

## *Meditative practices*

- Conscious breathing
  You can stop for a few moments and observe your breathing. Make it deeper, more complete. Straighten your back. Open your chest. Let the air fill all the spaces in you, from your belly to your head, passing through your lungs and bronchial tubes. Fill yourself with deep breathing. Then slowly let go of the air. Do it three times. You will see how your body oxygenates and revitalizes your brain. It helps you to slow down your mental speed and come back to the present moment.
- Minute of silence
  Every one or two hours, stop a minute and listen to the silence. Let the mental chatter stop and let the silence in.
- Full attention
  Set yourself a little while each day to practise being fully attentive and alert to what you think, feel, say, do, and to what happens around you.
- Intention
  Each morning you can meditate for fifteen minutes to connect to your intention for that day. Not your intention to attend to a client or students, or finish your list of things to do. Rather, your intention to live in your positive core. For example: "Today I will live with more joy", "I will see the glass half full", "I will keep my sense of humour".
- Process, digest and empty
  At the end of the working day it is good to do a meditation that helps to process the events of your day, digest what needs digesting and empty yourself of the unnecessary, of what isn't yours; it doesn't belong to you and you don't

need to be burdened by it.

### *Visualisation*

Meditation awakens the creative ability to work with images. This helps us to visualise using images that connect us to the positive core, to the essential values such as peace, love and freedom, and everything that provides us with well-being.

For example, visualise a sea open to a wide horizon, a solitary beach where your mind relaxes. Visualise a green field and the wind that keeps the air clean, and your mind refreshes itself. Look for images that inspire you and elevate you, those that connect you to pleasant emotions and fill you with a sense of well-being.

Learning to create visualisations helps us to connect to our dreams and keep them alive in our awareness.

# Bibliography

Boyatzis, Richard. "Coaching with Compassion: An fMRI Study of Coaching to the Positive or Negative Emotional Attractor"

Boyatzis, Richard. "Coaching with Compassion: Inspiring Health, Well-Being and Development in Organizations".

Bushe, Gervase R. "Appreciative Inquiry is Not (Just) about the Positive". Article published in *OD Practitioner*, vol. 39, nº. 4, pp 30–35

Caplan, Mariana. *Halfway Up the Mountain*, 1999

Cooperrider, David L.; Whitney, Diana; Trosten-Bloom, Amanda; Kaplin, Brian S. *Encyclopedia of Positive Questions, Vol. 1: Using Appreciative Inquiry to Bring Out the Best in Your Organization*, Lakeshore Communications: Euclid, Ohio, 2002

Cousins, Norman. *Human Options*, WW Norton and Co Inc.: Scranton, Pennsylvania, USA, 1988

d'Ors, Pablo. *Biografía del silencio*, Siruela, 2012

Dispenza, Joe. *Evolve Your Brain: The Science of Changing Your Mind*, Health Communications, Inc.: Deerfield Beach, Florida, USA, 2007

Fredrickson, Barbara. *Positivity*, Crown Publishing, Three Rivers Press: New York, 2009

Gergen, Kenneth J. *Towards Transformation in Social Knowledge*, Sage: London, 1994

Gergen, Kenneth J. *Relational Being: Beyond Self and Community*, Oxford University Press: New York, 2011

Gergen, Kenneth J. and Gergen, Mary. *Social Construction: Entering the Dialogue*, Taos Institute Publications, CSS Publishing Company: Chagrin Falls, Ohio, United States, 2004

Gergen, Kenneth J. and Gergen, Mary. *Reflexiones sobre la construcción social*, Paidós, Espasa Libros: Madrid, 2011

Goldberg, Marilee. *The Art of the Question: A Guide to Short-Term*

*Question-Centered Therapy*, 1997

Hanh, Thich Nhat. *Enseñanzas sobre el amor*, Ediciones Oniro, 1ª ed. Spanish version, 1998 (first in English 1997).

Kelm, Jaqueline Bascobert. *Appreciative Living: The Principles of Appreciative Inquiry in Personal Life*, Venet Publishers: Wake Forest, NC, 2005

Lyubomirsky, Sonja. *La ciencia de la felicidad*, Urano Ediciones: Barcelona, 2008

Orem, SL; Binkert, J. and Clancy, AL. *Appreciative Coaching: A Positive Process for Change*, Jossey-Bass: San Francisco, CA, 2007

Scharmer, Otto. *Theory U: Leading from the Future as It Emerges*, Society for Organizational Learning: Cambridge, MA, USA, 2007

Sloan, Barbara and Canine, Trudy. *AI Practitioner*, May 2007

Strano, Anthony. *Los cuatro movimientos*, Asociación Brahma Kumaris: Barcelona, 2010

Subirana, Miriam; Cooperrider, David. *Indagación Apreciativa: un enfoque innovador para la transformación personal y de las organizaciones*, Ed. Kairós: Barcelona, 2013

Subirana, Miriam. *La gran liberación, heartfulness y mindfulness*, Ed. Kairós: Barcelona, 2014

Subirana, Miriam. *El poder de nuestra presencia: una guía de coaching espiritual*, Ed. Kairós: Barcelona, 2012

Subirana, Miriam. *Serenidad mental: decide con lucidez*, Obelisco, 2011

Subirana, Miriam. *Atreverse a vivir: Reflexiones sobre el miedo, la valentía y la plenitud*. RBA: Barcelona, 2007. Republished 2014 in Biblioteca, Miriam Subirana, RBA: Barcelona.

Strano, Anthony. *Los cuatro movimientos*, Asociación Brahma Kumaris: Barcelona, 2010

Thatchenkery, Tojo. *Appreciative Intelligence: Seeing the Mighty Oak in the Acorn*, Berrett-Koehler Publishers: San Francisco, CA, 2006

Tschannen-Moran, Bob. "Five-principle coaching", article published in *AI Practitioner*, May 2007

Vogt, Eric E.; Brown, Juanita; Isaacs, David. *The Art of Powerful Questions: Catalyzing Insight, Innovation and Action*, Whole Systems Associates: California, 2003

Wheatley, MJ. *Leadership and the New Science*, Berrett-Koehler Communications, Inc.: San Francisco, CA, 1999

Whitney, Diana; Trosten-Bloom, Amanda. *The Power of Appreciative Inquiry*, Berrett-Koehler Publishers, Inc.: San Francisco, 2010

# Notes

1. Tojo Thatchenkery, *Appreciative Intelligence: Seeing the Mighty Oak in the Acorn,* Berrett-Koehler Publishers: San Francisco, CA, 2006
2. Javier Melloni, in the Prologue of Miriam Subirana's book, *Creativity to Reinvent Your Life: Reflections on Change, Intuition and Spiritual Alchemy,* O-Books: Ropley, Hants, UK, 2010
3. Pablo d'Ors, *Biografía del silencio,* Siruela, 2012, p 91
4. Paragraphs extracted from the article I published in *El País Semanal,* 13th April 2014, with the title "Acoger el sufrimiento".
5. Pablo d'Ors, 2012
6. Part of this section is extracted from the book by Subirana and Cooperrider, *Indagación Apreciativa: un enfoque innovador para la transformación personal y de las organizaciones,* Ed. Kairós: Barcelona, 2013
7. Sonja Lyubomirsky, *La ciencia de la felicidad,* Urano Ediciones: Barcelona, 2008
8. Jiddu Krishnamurti, *Afortunado el hombre que no es,* p 255
9. Miguel Ruiz, *Los cuatro acuerdos: una guía práctica para la libertad personal*
10. Text taken in great measure from the book *From Neediness to Fulfillment: Beyond Relationships of Dependence,* O-Books: UK, 2013. Original title: *Cómplices, más allá de las relaciones de dependencia,* published by RBA in 2010, and published again in the Biblioteca, Miriam Subirana of the RBA, in 2016.
11. Wendy Bristol, *Sin pareja y feliz: Cómo pasarlo en grande sin la otra mitad*
12. Jiddu Krishnamurti, *Sobre las relaciones,* p 30
13. Jiddu Krishnamurti, *Sobre las relaciones,* p 30
14. Nathaniel Branden, *Los Seis Pilares de La Autoestima,* p 327
15. Kenneth J. Gergen, "Toward a Relational Humanism",

*Journal of Humanistic Counseling,* 2015
16. Kenneth J. Gergen and Mary Gergen, *Social Construction: Entering the Dialogue,* Taos Institute Publications, 2004
17. Kenneth J. Gergen, *Towards Transformation in Social Knowledge,* Sage: London, 1994
18. Kenneth J. Gergen, "Toward a Relational Humanism", *Journal of Humanistic Counseling,* 2015
19. Subirana and Cooperrider, *Indagación Apreciativa: un enfoque innovador para la transformación personal y de las organizaciones,* Ed. Kairós; Barcelona, 2013, from the prologue by David Cooperrider, p 14
20. Subirana and Cooperrider, *Indagación Apreciativa: un enfoque innovador para la transformación personal y de las organizaciones,* Ed. Kairós, Barcelona, 2013
21. Part of this chapter is taken from the book: Subirana and Cooperrider, *Indagación Apreciativa: un enfoque innovador para la transformación personal y de las organizaciones,* Ed. Kairós: Barcelona, 2013
22. Kenneth J. Gergen, "Toward a Relational Humanism", *Journal of Humanistic Counseling,* 2015
23. Boyatzis, Richard, "Coaching with Compassion: an fMRI Study of Coaching to the Positive or Negative Emotional Attractor" and in "Coaching with Compassion: Inspiring Health, Well-Being and Development in Organizations".
24. Liz Roffe, Katja Schmidt, and Edzard Ernst. "A systematic review of guided imagery as an adjuvant cancer therapy". Article first published online: 13th January 2005. DOI: 10.1002/pon.889. Copyright © 2005 John Wiley & Sons, Ltd. *Psycho-Oncology.* Volume 14, Issue 8, pages 607–617, August 2005. Cited by Boyatzis in his articles mentioned in note 23.
25. Orem, SL; Binkert, J. and Clancy, AL, *Appreciative Coaching: A Positive Process for Change,* Jossey-Bass: San Francisco, CA, 2007, p 26

26. Fredrickson, Barbara L. *Positivity*, 2009, pp 8–11
27. Bob Tschannen-Moran, "Five-principle coaching", article published in *AI Practitioner*, May 2007, p 20
28. Sloan, Barbara; Canine, Trudy, "Appreciative Inquiry in Coaching: Exploration and Learnings". Article published in *AI Practitioner*, 2007, p 3
29. Margaret Wheatley, "Servant-Leadership and Community Leadership in the 21st Century", Inaugural lecture, The Robert K. Greenleaf Center for Servant Leadership annual conference, June 1999, p 35ff. Cited by Tschannen-Moran, article cited in note 16, p 21.
30. Fredrickson, Barbara, "Ampliar y construir a través de las emociones positivas". Transcription of a recording in 2002, at the conference of Positive Psychology.
31. Whitney, D. and Trosten-Bloom, A. (2003) "The power of Appreciative Inquiry". Published in the *AI Handbook* by David Cooperrider et al., pp 27–30
32. Sloan, Barbara; Canine, Trudy, "Appreciative Inquiry in Coaching: Exploration and Learnings". Article published in *AI Practitioner*, 2007, p 2
33. This chapter is an extract from the chapter: "El poder transformador de las preguntas", published in Subirana and Cooperrider, *Indagación Apreciativa: un enfoque innovador para la transformación personal y de las organizaciones*, Ed. Kairós: Barcelona, 2013.
34. Cooperrider, David L.; Whitney, Diana; Trosten-Bloom, Amanda; Kaplin, Brian S. *Encyclopedia of Positive Questions, Vol. 1: Using Appreciative Inquiry to Bring Out the Best in Your Organization*, Lakeshore Communications: Euclid, Ohio, 2002
35. Gervase R. Bushe, "Appreciative Inquiry is Not (Just) about the Positive". Article published in *OD Practitioner*, vol. 39, nº 4, pp 30–35.
36. Anthony Strano, *Los cuatro movimientos*, Asociación Brahma Kumaris: Barcelona, 2010

37. Sloan and Canine, op.cit. in note 28
38. Orem, SL; Binkert, J. and Clancy, AL, *Appreciative Coaching: A Positive Process for Change*, Jossey-Bass: San Francisco, CA, 2007, pp 214–218
39. Boyatzis, articles cited in note 23
40. Luke Younge, "Destiny in Appreciative Coaching: Appreciative Process as Action Planning", published in his blog, August 2014
41. Luke Younge, op.cit.
42. Boyatzis, articles cited in note 23
43. De Quattro, V.; Feng, M. "The sympathetic nervous system: the muse of primary hypertension". *J Hum Hypertens* 2002; 16 suppl 1: S64–9. Cited by Boyatzis, articles cited in note 23.
44. Barsade, Sigal G. and Gibson, Donald E., "Why Does Affect Matter in Organizations?" (2007). *Academy of Management Perspectives*, Vol. 21(1), pp 36–59. Cited in articles by Boyatzis, mentioned in note 23.
45. Schiller, Holland and Riley, *Appreciative Leaders: In the Eye of the Beholder*, TAOS Institute, 2001 (ISBN 0-9712312-0-6)
46. Whitney, Trosten-Bloom and Rader, *Appreciative Leadership*, McGraw-Hill, 2010 (ISBN 978-0-07-171406-8), p 3
47. Subirana and Cooperrider (2013), pp 129–146
48. Diana Whitney and Amanda Trosten-Bloom, "Five Strategies of Appreciative Leadership", published in *AI Practitioner*, Vol. 13, February 2011, p 43
49. Figure created by Joep C. de Jong for his presentation for the Dutch Society of Psychologists, May 2014.
50. David L. Cooperrider et al. *Encyclopedia of Positive Questions, Vol. 1: Using Appreciative Inquiry to Bring Out the Best in Your Organization*, Lakeshore Communications: Euclid, Ohio, 2002
51. http://www.greatplacetowork.com
52. These are 4 of the 9 practices that Joep C. de Jong defines in his lecture: "Ideas on global appreciative leadership", for the

Dutch Society of Psychologists, May 2014.

53. Subirana and Cooperrider (2013), on Líder servidor, p 134
54. Federico Mayor Zaragoza, prologue from Subirana, *El poder de nuestra presencia: una guía de coaching espiritual*, Ed. Kairós: Barcelona, 2012, pp 12–15
55. Boyatzis, articles cited in note 23
56. Parts of this chapter are taken from Subirana, *El poder de nuestra presencia: una guía de coaching espiritual*, Ed. Kairós: Barcelona, 2012
57. Thich Nhat Hanh, *Enseñanzas sobre el amor*, Ediciones Oniro, 1ª edition, p 32
58. Text on guilt is from the book *La gran liberación, heartfulness y mindfulness*, by the author. Ed. Kairós: Barcelona, 2014
59. Text taken from the book by Miriam Subirana and Ramón Ribalta, *Quién manda en tu vida? Reflexiones sobre la soberanía personal*, RBA, last edition, 2014, in the Biblioteca Miriam Subirana. Published in English by O-Books, *Who Rules in Your Life? Reflections on Personal Power*, 2008, London.
60. Extracted from the book *La gran liberación*, by Miriam Subirana, Ed. Kairós, 2014
61. Norman Cousins, *The Healing Heart: Antidotes to Panic and Helplessness*, 1983, p 205
62. Joe Dispenza, *Evolve Your Brain: The Science of Changing Your Mind*, Health Communications, Inc.: Deerfield Beach, Florida, USA, 2007
63. Otto Scharmer, "Addressing the Blind Spot of Our Time", an Executive Summary of the new book by Otto Scharmer, *Theory U: Leading from the Future as It Emerges*, Society for Organizational Learning: Cambridge, MA, USA, 2007, pp 2 and 3
64. Boyatzis, articles cited in note 23

BOOKS

O is a symbol of the world, of oneness and unity; this eye represents knowledge and insight. We publish titles on general spirituality and living a spiritual life. We aim to inform and help you on your own journey in this life.

**Visit our website: http://www.o-books.com**

**Find us on Facebook:**

**https://www.facebook.com/OBooks**

**Follow us on Twitter: @obooks**

**If you have enjoyed this book, why not tell other readers by posting a review on your preferred booksite?**
**Recent bestsellers from O-Books are:**

**Heart of Tantric Sex**
Diana Richardson
Revealing Eastern secrets of deep love and intimacy to Western couples.
Paperback: 978-1-90381-637-0
e-book: 978-1-84694-637-0

**Crystal Prescriptions**
The A-Z guide to over 1,200 symptoms and their healing crystals
Judy Hall
The first in the popular series of four books, this handy little guide is packed as tight as a pill-bottle with crystal remedies for ailments.
Paperback: 978-1-90504-740-6
e-book: 978-1-84694-629-5

**Take Me To Truth**
Undoing the Ego
Nouk Sanchez, Tomas Vieira
The best-selling step-by-step book on shedding the Ego, using the teachings of A Course In Miracles.
Paperback: 978-1-84694-050-7
e-book: 978-1-84694-654-7

**7 Myths about Love...Actually!**
The The journey from your HEAD to the HEART of your SOUL
Mike George
Smashes all the myths about LOVE.

Paperback: 978-1-84694-288-4
e-book: 978-1-84694-682-0

**The Holy Spirit's Interpretation of the New Testament**
A course in Understanding and Acceptance
Regina Dawn Akers
Following on from the strength of A Course in Miracles, NTI teaches us how to experience the love and oneness of God.
Paperback: 978-1-84694-085-9
e-book: 978-1-78099-083-5

**The Message of A Course In Miracles**
A translation of the text in plain language
Elizabeth A. Cronkhite
A translation of A Course in Miracles into plain, everyday language for anyone seeking inner peace. The companion volume, Practicing a Course In Miracles, offers practical lessons and mentoring.
Paperback: 978-1-84694-319-5
e-book: 978-1-84694-642-4

**Rising in Love**
My Wild and Crazy Ride to Here and Now, with Amma, the Hugging Saint
Ram Das Batchelder
Rising in Love conveys an author's extraordinary journey of spiritual awakening with the Guru, Amma.
Paperback: 978-1-78279-687-9
e-book: 978-1-78279-686-2

**Thinker's Guide to God**
Peter Vardy
An introduction to key issues in the philosophy of religion.
Paperback: 978-1-90381-622-6

**Your Simple Path**
Find happiness in every step
Ian Tucker
A guide to helping us reconnect with what is really important in our lives.
Paperback: 978-1-78279-349-6
e-book: 978-1-78279-348-9

**Find more titles and sign up to our readers' newsletter at http://www.johnhuntpublishing.com/mind-body-spirit.**

**Follow us on Facebook at https://www.facebook.com/OBooks and Twitter at https://twitter.com/obooks.**

**Most titles are published in paperback and as an e-book. Paperbacks are available in physical bookshops. Both print and e-book editions are available online. Readers of e-books can click on the live links in the titles to order.**

9781785353765